Apostle John Speaks from Heaven: A Divine Revelation

Matthew Robert Payne

Sheldon T Bennett

Please visit http://personal-prophecy-today.com to sow into Matthew's writing ministry, to request a personal prophecy or life coaching, or to contact him.

Cover designed by akira007 at fiverr.com.

Edited by Lisa Thompson at www.writebylisa.com You can email Lisa at writebylisa@gmail.com for your editing needs.

Published by Revival Waves of Glory Books & Publishing PO Box 596 Litchfield, Illinois 62056 USA

Revival Waves of Glory Books & Publishing is committed to excellence in the publishing industry. Their website is www.revivalwavesofgloryministries.com Book design Copyright © 2017 by Revival Waves of Glory Books & Publishing. All rights reserved.

Paperback: 9781973211198

DEDICATION

I want to dedicate this book to one of my greatest fans, Mary Gibson. She has read many of my books and has plenty of good things to share with me. As an author, it's great to speak to someone who has read many of your books. Mary has patience and love for me. She knows that I am on a journey, and she not only supports me but prays for me and my future. Here is another book, Mary!

ACKNOWLEDGEMENTS

I want to thank my mother and father for all the love they have given me. I want to thank Jesus, the Father, and the Holy Spirit for being part of my life and for leading me. I want to thank all of my friends who love and support me. I want to thank Bill Vincent for publishing my book and the people who have sown into my ministry to make it possible for me to publish this book.

I want to thank you, the reader, for deciding to buy this book and for believing in me enough to read it.

Finally, I want to thank John the Apostle for coming down and being interviewed. I have suffered some attacks from the enemy for the answers that he gave, but I guess that comes with the territory.

Table of Contents

PART 1: MY QUESTIONS

CHAPTER 1
How do you feel about being here today?

First of all, let me say that it is a real honor to come and speak with you today, Matthew.

I really admire a few things about you. First, you are courageous like the Lord commanded Joshua to be. You are bold, and you do what the Lord commissions and inspires you to do via the Holy Spirit. He leads you to do everything that he asks you to do.

The idea to interview me in this book came from a visit in heaven where you actually talked to me in one of your meetings with the galactic council. You will address this further in your book, *My Visits to the Galactic Council: Book 2*, which is not published yet. In your interaction with the saints, I asked you if I could be your next interview, and you agreed. We know that everything in heaven operates by the direction of the Holy Spirit.

You agreed to interview me, so here we are. It is great to see your obedience and willingness to follow the Holy Spirit. I also love it that you are so giving of your time and your resources, your love and your patience. You are very understanding of people. You are very devoted to training and equipping people, and you spend your whole life earning money and allowing people to give money to your ministry so that you can produce more and more books. None of the money is really spent on yourself. You just keep on writing books. You don't produce books for profit, and your book-writing ministry takes a loss. You do it all for the glory of God.

First and foremost, you are really concerned about the glory of the Lord. You want to see the Name of Jesus lifted up and glorified in the earth. Because of your obedience and with your love and your giving attitude, I am here to give to you today. I am here to spend some time with you, answering the questions that you have for me and addressing the topics that you have prepared for me to discuss. Then, I will continue and answer the questions that your friend, Sheldon, asked.

When I have answered all your questions and you have reviewed the typing and corrected them, then Sheldon will post a response and a reflection on each of the answers that I give to his questions. This should turn out to be a wonderful book that encourages, edifies, and equips the Church. It will build up people, instruct them, direct them, and give them understanding. It will be all of these beneficial things as inspired by the Holy Spirit.

I have a copy of the book in my hands. If you look into your living room now, I have a copy of the book that you have produced in my hands. I am talking about six or eight weeks in the future when the book has been edited professionally and readied for publishing. I have a copy of your book that has been produced in the future here in my hands if your readers can receive it.

This interview will be edited by you. Sheldon will contribute more reflections, and then you will edit what Sheldon says. The editor will then edit what both of you say. She will review it three times, and the final product will be produced into a book. You will be inspired for a cover design. Eventually, the book will be published and made available. I have the book from the future, and I am waving it here.

I have actually seen all of the books that you have written in your life. I can see twenty to thirty years in the future, and I can see every book that you have ever written. If you look around in your living room, you can see a bookshelf that is lined with many books. These are the books that you are producing over the next twenty to thirty years of your life. You will impact thousands of lives as an author.

We know how many people you will reach and how many people this book will reach. We know who will actually read this book.

If you are reading this book and this introduction right now, rest assured that I am in your house watching you. I am with you, wherever you are reading this book or wherever you are traveling. I am watching you read this introduction. I am here, looking over you as you read.

It's a real honor and a privilege to be here. I've known this was going to happen for years before these events unfolded.

Everything that is said has been orchestrated and directed by God. No matter what is said, the content will be cleaned up, then edited, and given more clarity to produce the book that I hold in my hand.

People don't have to worry that the book will be edited and copy edited. It will just be made better and clearer. The editor will correct my grammar or rephrase any wording that needs to be cleaned up. My sign of approval will be on everything that has been said. The final edition of the book has been released, accepted, and approved by God.

It's an honor to be here. I really love you, Matthew. I could go on with dozens of characteristics that I love about your life. I just mentioned a couple here. But it's a real privilege to be in your house. In the next few hours, I hope to bring you a lot of fresh insight and revelation on the topics that we will cover.

Comments from Sheldon:

I am simply elated and humbled to have the opportunity to contribute to this book and would like to note that even as Matthew asked me to help him that John was sitting in Matthews's living room while we were on the phone. It was surreal, and the Spirit was poignant and tangible even in my little room in the camp where I reside while I am working in the north. I live north of Lake Eden and am constantly reminded that I live on the sides of the north. The city where I lived most of my life is alternately called Gateway to the North.

The manifestation of God's Kingdom came into my life after tragedies. God was watching over me and used his great grace to catapult me from intellectual knowledge of the Lord and his Kingdom to seeing it manifest before my eyes.

About four years ago, I asked the Lord if I could one day co-write or participate in one of Matthews's books. I have found that today, God still answers prayers. This is truly beyond what I could ever have hoped or thought.

When the Lord first showed me Matthew and shortly thereafter connected us, I never knew that we would have the opportunity to work together like this. The Lord had me interceding for people like Matthew and others in his situation. God is taking people from the highways and byways and putting them in seats that were left empty in that great hall. Those who were supposed to be at the wedding feast were too busy and too enamored by the opportunities in their lives. Instead, they were focused on making money and adding prestige to their own kingdoms.

I had a vision a while ago of someone reading one of Matthews's books and as they read, I was seeing the book as if it were spilling light all over their room. An entourage from heaven was coming through to minister to them and to bring more of the kingdom of heaven into their lives.

When I read this introduction by John, it was like déjà vu as if I had read it before. John, you have always been one of my favorite followers of Jesus. Your writings have inspired and helped me, and I am sure others, to survive many attacks on our faith and even on our lives while I walked the path to become the son of God I always wanted to be.

So much is happening to bring the manifestation of heaven to earth—to open up people's homes and lives to the dynamics of heaven having its way here. We pray it all the time. "Thy Kingdom come, thy will be done, on earth as it is in heaven" (Matthew 6:10, KJV). So be it.

I have sung the following song for years, asking the Lord's Kingdom to come and demonstrate itself through us. Make this your prayer as well.

Take My Life and Let It Be

Frances Ridley Havergal

Take my life and let it be
Consecrated, Lord, to Thee.
Take my moments and my days,
Let them flow in endless praise.

Take my hands and let them move
At the impulse of Thy love.
Take my feet and let them be
Swift and beautiful for Thee.

Take my voice and let me sing,
Always, only for my King.
Take my lips and let them be
Filled with messages from Thee.

Take my silver and my gold,
Not a mite would I withhold.
Take my intellect and use
Every power as Thou shalt choose.

Take my will and make it Thine,
It shall be no longer mine.

Take my heart, it is Thine own,
It shall be Thy royal throne.

Take my love, my Lord, I pour
At Thy feet its treasure store.
Take myself and I will be
Ever, only, all for Thee.[1]

---

[1] *Hymnary*. 2017. "Take My Life and Let It Be." Public domain.
http://hymnary.org/text/take_my_life_and_let_it_be

CHAPTER 2
What do you like about Jesus?

Jesus is one of my favorite subjects. "What could be a more favorite subject?" you might ask. Well, the Bride of Christ is also one of my favorite subjects. Jesus knows who he is, and he is sure and confident of who he is. He's beautiful in every way, but the bride and the people who know Jesus don't know him as well as they should, and they don't know who they are in Christ. They don't know their identity as Christians.

I tremendously love Christians and the Bride of Christ, but what I love about Jesus is that he is so understanding. You have to consider that when Jesus walked on earth, he wasn't filled with all the knowledge of God. He was a human that was led by the power of the Holy Spirit. Now in heaven, Jesus knows everything. With his knowledge of everything, Jesus is so understanding and patient with people.

You might know Jesus as a person or an entity that seems harsh, full of rules, and full of regulations. You might see those things in Jesus. However, I don't see him like that and have not experienced him in that way. You might know Jesus as the Jesus who rebuked the Pharisees and Jesus who tore up the temple with a whip and whipped money changers and beat people on the back. You might believe in an angry Jesus.

Well, the Jesus that I know is all loving, all patient, and all understanding. I really love the fact that Jesus knows the end from the beginning. Like I said, I'm sitting here with bookcases full of books right in front of you that you've written over the next thirty years. If you went up and looked closely in the spirit, you could see the titles and you could sit down and list them all. You'd know what you will write books about and the subjects that you will cover.

I've been in the future sixty years, in fact, to even write the book of Revelation. I've seen the future for what could be at least a thousand years after Jesus ruled on earth. But Jesus has been to the end. If there is an end to eternity, it is a long way, and he knows where we are all going. He knows the job that he is doing in each of our lives. As people in heaven and people on earth, he knows your end, and he knows where you will end up. He is all loving and all patient, and he is understanding.

He knows the very sin that you struggle with. He knows the months and the years that you have been struggling with a particular sin in your life, and he understands when you will find the healing in your life that will allow you to be set free from that sin.

He understands that some people will never conquer sin, and they will struggle with sin until the day they die. They will continue confessing their sin before Jesus and never be really set free because of their bondage to pain and demons and other issues in their lives. Some people go to churches without the necessary facilities or the information and capacity to set people free.

Jesus understands you and me. He understands the progression of people in heaven and how they are learning and going from glory to glory. He understands where you are at. If you are struggling with something, he understands why you struggle. He understands who hurt you and what caused the pain and wounds in your life to make you struggle.

He knows that people are trying to do their best even those described as wicked people in the Bible. A wicked person is someone like an illegal slave trader. He understands the motivations behind their hearts to make them do what they do when they commit evil acts.

Jesus is completely understanding. He has all knowledge. He has knowledge of your past and of everything you have been through. He has knowledge of your whole future. He knows what sort of person you are going to be in a thousand years as we enter into eternity. He knows everything about you. That's what I love about Jesus. He is understanding and knowledgeable with the patience, compassion, and the love to see you through to the end.

I really loved that about Jesus when I knew him on earth. I really loved the fact that when he looked at you, you could see that he knew you. Even on earth, when you looked at Jesus, you could see eternity in his eyes. You could see a depth of compassion that you had never encountered before.

I am not sure if many of you readers have experienced the look of love in the eyes of Jesus. I'm not sure if many of you readers had a vision or met Jesus face to face, but Jesus has an amazing capacity to love. When you experience a look in his eyes, when you experience him looking at you like Princess Diana explains in *Princess Diana Speaks from Heaven: A Divine Revelation*, you are undone.

When Jesus looks into your eyes with his love, he will just undo you. You are just undone by the love that he shares, especially the resurrected Jesus in heaven, who is totally walking in the Spirit, who is totally God. God was formerly a human as Jesus and walked through life as a human with a human intellect but not the mind of God.

What I love about Jesus is not only that he's understanding but that he is full of compassion with the ability to be patient and wait for you to progress on earth and even after you are in heaven. When Jesus was on earth, he understood me. He had divine revelation about what I was going to achieve in my future on earth. He saw visions of me. He knew I was going to be important. He knew that I was going to write my gospel and my letters and the book of Revelation. He knew that my book of Revelation was going to impact churches up until the modern day.

He knew many people were going to be brought into the kingdom through my gospel of John, which many theologians will tell you is the best gospel out of the four gospels. Many evangelical people will hand out the gospel of John when they witness, knowing that a person can be brought into a relationship with Jesus by simply having and reading the gospel of John. Jesus knew me on earth. He really knew me. He understood my past and my future. He understood where I was when I was with him, and he understood everything about me. Jesus's understanding can't be underestimated.

You live in a world, dear reader, where people don't fully understand you, and even the people who seem to understand you want you to conform to their ways and their standards. Many people seem to tread a path that develops friendships, and they have relationships with their family. Those people that become close to them might try and mold them and direct them and control their lives and hopes. Sometimes it seems that a total stranger will understand you and accept you even better than the people who know you the best. That situation is true for your friends, Mary, Andrea, and Wendy.

Jesus addressed this in Mark 6:4 when he said, "A prophet is not without honor except in his own country, among his own relatives, and in his own house." Jesus was saying that the people who know you best won't accept that you're a prophet. Jesus was saying that a prophet will be known by his gift and his anointing and his message by total strangers and respected by them but not among people he loves. For more on this subject, see Matthew's book, *Deep Calls unto Deep*.

Jesus understands you more completely than anyone else, more completely than me, and more completely than the saints. Matthew regularly interacts with saints, but not even saints have the understanding of Jesus. I understand Matthew very well, but I don't understand him to the depths that Jesus understands him.

Jesus understands you perfectly. I know I'm continuing on the subject of understanding, but it's so important in this world where everyone fights to have a voice on Facebook and fights to be promoted and accepted and recognized for who they are. It's so important in this world to be understood. So many problems in this world exist because people and people groups are not understood as they should be. There are so many divisions and so much disunity. There are so many factions. The U.S. is so divided because of a lack of understanding.

Understanding is crucial. Jesus is a man who understands. He understands the Word of God, understands the world, understands the future, and understands the past. He is just amazing. He won't tell you something that will harm you, so he might not tell you about your future. He might not tell you that you're going to produce a book because you might get nervous and run away from the task like Jonah ran away when he was sent to or asked to warn Nineveh. Jesus might not tell you your future, but he understands your future, and he understands you. Jesus is really patient, and he's kind. He's loving. He's exceptionally good at directing lives and positioning people to be their very best.

There's so much I could say about Jesus. I could spend an hour talking about him. I could spend fifty pages talking about different dimensions of Jesus and different parts of him and what I like about him. I love Jesus because he is a man of understanding. Like I've said before, and I'll repeat again, he understands the world. He understands the world's past and future. He understands the Word of God. He understands me and you. He understands what you need to know now and what you need to know about your future. He understands what it will take to get you to your future. He understands what sin you are in now. He understands what sin will control you in the future. He understands the day you'll break free of certain sins. He understands everything. He understands completely.

Jesus is a man of understanding. Many will come to him one day and say, “Lord, we did great signs and wonders. We did this in your name, and we did that in your name.” And Jesus will say to them, “Depart from me. You never understood me.” Now, that's a little different than what the scripture says, but that's a more complete rendering. “You never understood me. You never knew me. I never knew you. We never had a relationship” (See Matthew 7:21-23).

Jesus is a man of understanding. You need to focus on him. You need to set it as your task to come to understand what Jesus taught, what Jesus commanded, who Jesus was, what sort of person Jesus is, and model your life after him. You need to start to walk and behave like Jesus did on earth. You might want to act like we did on earth—like I did, like Peter and Paul did. We reached a stage where we lived a life that was—some might say it's blasphemous—free from sin. We lived in resurrection power. We lived in bodies that were formed in the new creation with the resurrection power of Jesus Christ. These are some things that I loved about Jesus.

CHAPTER 3
What do you like about heaven?

If you've read the book, *Great Cloud of Witnesses Speak*, nineteen saints speak about what they like about heaven. Several saints speak about what they like in heaven in the following books with their names: *Michael Jackson Speaks from Heaven*, *Mary Magdalene Speaks from Heaven*, and *Princess Diana Speaks from Heaven*. Many of us have already spoken through Matthew, and he has compiled and edited books about what we have to say that we like about heaven. I hope you can read these books for more information about heaven.

Heaven is constantly evolving. It's moving. It's getting better. How do you improve on perfection? How do you improve on earth? Doesn't earth improve by new discoveries, new creations, and new ways of doing things that come about through others? Earth evolves and becomes more efficient as people are inspired with new ideas that often come from heaven. Heaven expands, improves, and becomes better, more efficient, and more remarkable through the ideas of the people of heaven.

People don't often mention the following fact that I love about heaven. Matthew has interviewed many saints who explain that heaven is getting ready to invade earth. The people of heaven, the saints of heaven, the population of heaven are gearing up to visit, interact with, encounter, walk, counsel, and mentor people on earth.

Over the coming ten to twenty to thirty years on earth, many people, thousands and thousands of Christians, will start encountering visitations from Jesus, visitations from heaven, heaven's angels, and visitations from saints on earth and saints in heaven that know their past, their future, and everything about them. Heaven will start to co-labor with the people of earth to help earth perfect itself, turn itself around, and become a habitation for perfection.

The people of heaven are eagerly waiting to speak to the people of earth to counsel and direct them. We play films in heaven about the future of earth. We show people in heaven the future of earth, and we inspire them on how they're going to counsel, direct, and mentor people on earth so that heaven can invade earth and so that the culture in heaven can come down and transform earth. We're excited about that. I like that aspect of heaven. Matthew is just a forerunner who's interviewing saints from heaven, and he seems to have an assignment from God to bring heaven to earth and give our people information, knowledge, and wisdom from heaven through the saints and the interviews.

Heaven looks forward to days and years where the people of earth and the people in heaven run competitions with each other. Heaven and earth will be competing to strive for excellence in certain areas and ways. On the new earth, when Jesus is reigning and when sinners have been eradicated, earth will be in a competition with heaven, and heaven and earth will compete.

Saints from heaven will come down and walk on earth, and saints from earth will be able to go up and walk in heaven. It will be two-way; living saints, people who have never died, will be able to go up to heaven and walk through heaven, interact with heaven, and come back to earth. People from heaven will be able to walk on earth in fleshly bodies and interact with people on earth just like Jesus came from the Father and interacted with the people on earth.

He walked through a wall and ate a meal with the disciples. Thomas put a finger in his side and proved that he had a spear run through him. Thomas was a doubter, and Jesus knew his words of doubt, and he told Thomas not to doubt and asked him to put his finger in his side (John 20:27). Jesus ate fish on the beach with the disciples after he'd been resurrected (John 21:13). Jesus had a real body of flesh on earth. Saints can appear in visions, but in the future, saints will walk on earth in what appears to be bodies of flesh and interact in an encounter just like Jesus in his resurrected body.

We enjoy encountering the people of earth. We hope that all the readers of the book burn with hunger and want to interact with the people of heaven. Heaven is an exciting place without sin, envy, strife, anger, maliciousness, drunkenness, lust, envy, murder, or any type of sin at all—any sin that you can think of, none of that exists in heaven. Imagine a place where nothing is wrong and where nothing can go wrong. You can't stub your toe. You can't fall over and be injured. You can't hurt yourself. You can't be sick. You can't grow old. Your body won't decay.

Everything is perfect, yet even in this perfection, it gets better in earth time. Heaven operates in a sort of time, but in earthly time, everything improves every week and every month in heaven. The saints of heaven are creating and co-laboring with God to create a more interesting, more fully functioning heaven for the rest of the people.

I like the fact that Jesus and the Father are celebrated in heaven, that Jesus is given supreme glory in heaven, that the Father is not afraid to glorify his Son.

Some people relate more closely to Jesus because they had wounding in their lives with father figures. They might take a while in heaven to even warm up to God, but people in heaven sometimes come there without knowing God at all. Yet, one look, one embrace from the Father can just heal so much and bring a person so far.

The Father is so amazing. It's unbelievable to have a relationship with the Father of creation, the God of Jesus, the Father of Jesus. It's so rewarding and beautiful to be hugged and held by God. It fills you with ecstasy.

God loves everyone. He has a side of justice to him, but everyone in heaven is loved by the Father. Jesus is the groom—the groom of the bride. Everyone in heaven is divinely and spiritually matched with Jesus. He is the darling of heaven. It's hard to put into English words how remarkable Jesus is.

Princess Diana, in *Princess Diana Speaks from Heaven: A Divine Revelation*, speaks really well and gives a great description of the Jesus of heaven. If you want a good look at Jesus, I really recommend that you buy all of the books that Matthew recommended in this book for ninety-nine cents each. He has no problem when the saints recommend his books as resources, but I especially recommend that you read the book about Jesus.

Jesus lives outside of time; he has seen all the presidents of the United States right up until his return to bring the church home. He knows who wins the 2020 and the 2024 elections in America. He has seen the future of America and if they follow the course that directs them toward God or if they choose a different course that takes them into darkness and away from God.

Jesus understands the world. He understands the people of heaven. He has tremendous understanding, and here I go again, talking about the understanding of Jesus. He's incomprehensible to describe.

How do you capture a symphony in words? How do you explain a symphony? Even someone who hears a symphony can hear it better and more exquisitely if they have an understanding of music and of how music is constructed and orchestrated. Someone who is trained in music could be trained to conduct the symphony or even to write a symphony. There are different levels of everything.

Understanding Jesus in mere English words is like trying to explain what a symphony sounds like in words, which is hard to capture. You really need to meet Jesus. I recommend that you read books like *Seeing in the Spirit Made Simple* by Praying Medic and books by Matthew Robert Payne about different subjects, including heaven.

The Jesus of heaven is a darling. You know how a young male will have a female, and he'll do anything to please the female to the point where the female accepts his hand in marriage. Jesus is like a bride to a male. Jesus is the ultimate catch and the ultimate groom of heaven. I know I am mixing metaphors here, but Jesus is the ultimate catch.

Jesus shared a parable about the pearl of great price in Matthew 13:45-46. In one understanding of the parable of the pearl of great price, you can say that the pearl trader went and traded all his pearls, all his earthly possessions, for money to buy the pearl of great price. Jesus is that pearl of great price. You should spend your whole life and everything that's in you to possess more of him, to possess him. To possess him is so amazing. The more you can possess him on earth before you die, the more that you can be intimate with him on earth before you die, will make your time in heaven so much more exquisite and beneficial.

I had a tremendous relationship with Jesus on earth, and in heaven, my relationship went from glory to glory. The Jesus of heaven is amazing. No one outside of God or the Holy Spirit could match or come to grips with his knowledge and wisdom. He is beyond comprehension. 1 Corinthians 2:16 asks, "Who can understand the mind of God? But we have the mind of Christ" (loose paraphrase). It's a wonderful, wonderful experience to spend your time with Jesus Christ.

CHAPTER 4
Coming out of the world

We explained in the last chapter that it's a whole lot more beneficial in heaven for you if you have a wonderful relationship with Jesus Christ before you come to heaven. A few steps are involved in developing an intimate relationship with Jesus on earth before you come to heaven. Matthew has a book called *7 Keys to Intimacy with Jesus* that explains essential keys to developing a relationship with Jesus.

In this chapter, I want to focus on a passage in 1 John 2:15-17 (NLT) and unpack it a bit.

"Do you not love the world nor the things it offers you, for when you love the world, you do not have to love the Father in you. For the world offers only a craving for physical pleasure, a craving for everything we see, and a pride in our achievements and possessions. These are not from the Father, but are from this world. And this world is fading away, along with everything that people crave. But anyone who does what pleases God will live forever."

Please note my last words. Anyone who does what pleases God will live forever. The following are all religious acts: going to church, putting your coins in the offering plate, praying to Jesus, going to a weekly Bible study, and reading the Bible. Certainly, they are Christian actions, but you can totally serve everything of the world and still do these things.

You can do all of the following and still be serving the world:

- Read the Bible
- Go to church
- Pray one-way prayers to God
- Go to weekly Bible studies and
- Tithe.

When I wrote this passage to the church, I was saying, "Do not love the things of the world." If you love the world and everything about the world, if you love the things of the world, then you don't possess the love of the Father in you. When I warn you not to do these things, I'm saying that if you do these things, you aren't doing what pleases the Father. It should be easy to understand that if you love the world and the things of the world, you won't be doing the things that please the Father.

What are some things of the world? Of course, you need a job in this world to survive. Is it wrong to have a job? No. There's nothing wrong with having a job.

Is there anything wrong with having a car? No. Sometimes a person needs a car to get to certain places: work, church, and different events. Families need a car. Obviously, it's hard to do the shopping and run the children to school and go to work if you don't have a car. Some families even need two cars.

There's nothing wrong with owning a couple of cars or a house. There's nothing wrong with having a job. However, you should not focus on having a nice car, a nice house, nice possessions, or brand-name clothes. There's a real difference between spending money on what pleases your flesh and spending money on what pleases God.

David Servant, a pastor that Matthew knows, asked God once if he was doing or preaching anything in error. The Father told him that he loved the world too much, and he was teaching people that it is okay to serve the world and its lusts. He went through a process of down-sizing his house, his car, and even his clothes. He channeled that extra money that he saved into missions. Now, he runs a mission's organization called Heaven's Family that you can find on the internet. Millions of dollars go to these ministries, supporting poor Christians around the world and doing a tremendous amount of wonderful work.

How much could you give to the Lord and to ministries if you didn't want:

- The biggest and brightest house
- The newest and best car
- The latest phone
- The top computer or
- Brand-name clothes.

So many Christians in this world are sadly chasing after looking good and being dressed in brand-name clothes. Why do you even buy brand-name clothes? Is it because other people will recognize that you're wearing a Chanel jacket or carrying a Gucci bag? Other people will recognize, "Well, so, that's really cute and looks so classy. That's Chanel, so that person really has money."

What are we doing to actually dress ourselves as compared to impressing other people? Are you buying clothes to dress yourself so that you're not naked? Or are you buying clothes to impress other people? When you're buying a house, is it to keep the rain off your head, or is it to impress others? Who are you trying to impress?

Is your house a safe place for your family to grow? Or is your house more about impressing your neighbors and friends?

When you buy your car, are you buying a car that's the best and most functional car for your family? Or are you buying a car because you want to look good with the best brand of car so that you have a great reputation among your friends and neighbors?

Why did you accept that position at work? Do you want to take pride in your achievements and possessions? Do you take pride in your job? Is it more about what other people think when you put a title, such as doctor, apostle, or prophet, before your name? Is it about your title, or is it about serving God? Do you take pride in your possessions or in your achievements?

These things of the world sadly come naturally to you and to the people of the world. People usually want the nicest houses, cars, and possessions. They want the best brands. But is it about having the best brands that will function well, or is it about impressing other people? Is it about having pride?

I want to be very clear with you. The God that I serve in heaven is a God of abundance. I'm not saying that you can't have a luxury car. But if a car costs $70,000, and you can buy a car that does the same job for $20,000, wouldn't the $50,000 savings be better served in buying land and building churches for seven villages in India at $7,000 each for a church on land? Wouldn't housing a thousand Christians in India in churches (about 150 people per church) be more beneficial than your pride?

I want to ask you: is it okay to have luxury? It's okay to have the best. It's okay to have great cars, beautiful houses, and luxury. But do these things possess you? Are you spending millions on your house before you spend millions on the kingdom?

What proportion of your ministry spendings is your house when compared to your ministry? If your ministry is earning $15,000,000 a year, is it okay to have a $2,000,000 house? What if your ministry was only bringing in $2,000,000 annually, should you still have a $2,000,000 house? The answer somewhat depends on the proportion. Everything is fine if it doesn't possess you.

The problem with the world and its lusts is that people are geared toward pride in their achievements and possessions. This is why I spoke about worth. This passage is one of the most quoted passages by Matthew in his books. Matthew once asked Jesus if he would ever stop quoting this passage, and Jesus replied to him, "Not while other people are still lusting for the things of this world. It's one of the most important passages in the Bible."

I want to ask you this important question. Who owns you? Does the world own you? How is that working out for you? How is your relationship with the world? If you could save 50 percent of your income by not spending as much on possessions, what would 50 percent of your earnings do for missions?

For instance, it costs Matthew $2,000 or more to produce a book. What could you do with $2,000 to $2,500 savings of your income?

You could sponsor one of Matthew’s books that could touch hundreds or thousands of lives. So many things that don't cost a lot of money can be done for the kingdom. Many ministries have different things that you can do that will disciple a Christian or save a person.

My point on the matter is that when you're serving the world or the things of the world, when you're pursuing achievements and possessions, you're not serving Jesus. You can go to church and read your Bible. You can pray a one-way prayer. You can go to Bible studies and still be lukewarm. Jesus might still want to vomit you out of his mouth.

James 4:4 says that anyone who wants to become a friend of the world makes himself an enemy of God. You can go to church, read your Bible, pray one-way prayers, go to Bible studies, and still be an enemy of God if you are a friend of the world.

You have to choose for yourself, and this is a very tough message from a man who wrote this scripture. Choose for yourself this day who you will serve. (See Joshua 24:15.) Will you serve Jesus Christ, my Savior, the one who understands all things, or will you serve your belly and the lust of your flesh? Is the recognition of your family and your friends so important to you that you would make yourself ineffective in the world? Would you prefer to do what pleases God and live forever in heaven with much reward and much glory?

What will you choose? Do you choose a life of serving the world, or do you choose a life of serving God? It's time to really consider these factors. Let’s talk now about being lukewarm.

CHAPTER 5
Being lukewarm

I want to speak about another passage and talk about the church identified in the book of Revelation as the lukewarm church. Revelation 3:14-22 tells us:

"And to the angel of the church of the Laodiceans write, 'These things says the Amen, the Faithful and True Witness, the Beginning of the creation of God: "I know your works, that you are neither cold nor hot. I could wish you were cold or hot. So then, because you are lukewarm, and neither cold nor hot I will vomit you out of My mouth. Because you say, 'I am rich, have become wealthy, and have need of nothing'—and do not know that you are wretched, miserable, poor, blind, and naked—I counsel you to buy from Me gold refined in the fire, that you may be rich; and white garments, that you may be clothed, that the shame of your nakedness may not be revealed; and anoint your eyes with eye salve, that you may see. As many as I love, I rebuke and chasten. Therefore be zealous and repent. Behold, I stand at the door and knock. If anyone hears My voice and opens the door, I will come in to him and dine with him, and he with Me. To him who overcomes I will grant to sit with Me on My throne, as I also overcame and sat down with My Father on His throne. He who has an ear, let him hear what the Spirit says to the churches.'"

First of all, the word *repent* means *change your ways*. It doesn't mean simply telling God that you're sorry for your behavior. It means turning 180 degrees and starting to walk in the other direction. This was written by me but was a prophecy by Jesus, speaking to seven churches when I was living on earth two thousand years ago. However, it's very relevant now. It is part of the canon of scripture and certainly part of this book.

This passage refers to people who serve the world with the richest and most prestigious houses, the brand-name clothes, and the best positions, who have impressed all their friends and neighbors with their possessions and with all they've achieved. They are lukewarm.

They say that they're rich, wealthy, and have need of nothing. They do not know that they are wretched, miserable, poor, blind, and naked. The problem with the church, the problem with people who go to church, is that they don't see themselves as naked, poor, wretched, and miserable. Many Christians can't witness to another person or share the Gospel with others.

When you read *Michael Jackson Speaks from Heaven: a Divine Revelation*, *Mary Magdalene Speaks from Heaven: a Divine Revelation*, or *Princess Diana Speaks from Heaven: a Divine Revelation*, you'll find books that would be useful to give to one of your non-Christian friends because they might be very interested in reading what those people say. These are great evangelistic tools to give to your friends, but many Christians have no idea about how to witness to their friends simply because they are poor, blind, miserable, and naked.

Sadly, they really don't have much going on in their lives that is better than the people of the world. Many Christians are so busy serving the world and all its cravings that they are no better than the world themselves. Many churches don't move in healing, signs, wonders, and miracles. Many churches depend on doctors, specialists, and hospitals to heal their sick. They don't have people in their church that can heal. Why would the people of the world even want to come to your church?

Many churches are full of people arguing about different doctrines. People have no idea that they're poor in spirit. They have no idea that they're actually broke with no eternal rewards built up in heaven. They don't know that they could be experiencing Jesus every day, along with angels and saints. They could be experiencing prosperity with enough for a nice car and a spacious house. They would have enough for what they need. But there's not enough for lavishness or greed.

You could instead live a life with enough money coming in to not only supply your own needs but to give generously, hundreds and thousands of dollars to missions and to spread the gospel, which will last for eternity.

Do you know that if your money goes toward saving one person who becomes a Christian because of the investment that you made, that person lives for eternity in heaven? What price could you put on that? Does $5,000 or $10,000 or even $50,000 begin to cover it? Can you think of a friend or family member that you wouldn't pay $1,000 so that they could go to heaven? Do you have a friend or co-worker that you love? Do you have a relative that you love that's not a Christian? Would you give $5,000 to see him or her become a Christian?

The series of books *Divine Revelation* will all be designed to win your friends to Jesus. What would you do to see that happen? How much is it worth to you for one of your loved ones to be saved? Think if someone else spent $5,000 and one of the people that you loved was saved. How much would that be worth to you?

Do you know that you can live so that all your necessities are paid for and you then contribute thousands of dollars to save the lives of untold numbers of people? For example, if you saved $50,000 and did not buy a luxury car but instead bought a reliable vehicle for $20,000, that price difference alone could sponsor seven churches that would house a thousand Christians.

A thousand Christians could be out of the rain and out of their houses and meeting in a central worship place in a village in India. A thousand Christians could be blessed just because you chose not to buy that luxury car but to buy a much more reasonable car that would do the job. How will you live? What decisions will you make? How will you repent? How will you change?

Will you change? Maybe you will just think, “Matthew is just deluded. This isn't really the apostle John speaking.” Will you accept that it's really me speaking, saying that you need to change? You need to stop living according to the lust of the world and start living for Jesus.

You need to think of ways that you can save money so that you can invest in the kingdom. Jesus spoke in the parable about the talents and the minas. (See Matthew 25:14-30.) Both of the parables are similar. He spoke of how he gave a certain amount to certain man. In the parable of the talents, he gave one talent to one man, two talents to another man, and five talents to a third man. The man went away for a long time and then came back. The one that had had five talents gave him ten talents back because he had invested them or put them into business and made another five talents. He was rewarded.

The one that had two talents doubled it and made it into four, and he was rewarded. However, the one with one talent said that he knew the man was a hard master, so he'd hidden his talent and kept it safe. The master became really upset with him and said that he was a wicked servant. He gave his one talent to the man with ten talents.

Do you think that you were given an ability to work in a job with health, a family, skills, and intellect so that you could have an expensive house, a luxury car, and brand-name clothes? Do you think that God is here to give you your every desire? Or do you think that you've been given the ability to work and the intellect to hold down a job so that you could finance ministries and build the Kingdom of God and save more people?

Matthew spends his time writing books, educating Christians, and helping them become more effective and more intimate with Jesus. You can learn what Matthew teaches by spending $30.00 and buying thirty of his books for ninety-nine cents each. Read them for yourself and ask yourself, “Would I invest in Matthew?

Would I invest in one of his book projects or give a portion toward a book? Is he honestly interested in educating Christians and helping them to become more effective, more intimate, and more powerful in their relationship with Jesus and in the world?"

What about ministries like Joyce Meyer, Benny Hinn, Andrew Wommack, or Joseph Prince? What ministry do you admire? How can you support them with your finances? Isn't it more beneficial to support ministries and God with your money rather than spending it on your achievements and possessions? Jesus said in Luke 12:15 that life does not consist of an abundance of your possessions.

Like we said, Jesus said that the meaning of life isn't found in an abundance of possessions. When will we stop this fascination with owning things? There's not a person in the West who can't afford to give something to God, no matter how small. Everyone has a way to give to God. Even if you can't afford to give money to him, you can give of your time instead, which is valuable in the Kingdom of God.

The church and Christians have become ineffective because they're not serving the true God. One of the main hindrances to developing the type of intimate relationship with Jesus that you want if you're going to heaven is the fact that they're serving the world instead of serving God.

We haven't talked about being neither hot nor cold but Jesus said that he would vomit the lukewarm person out of his mouth. I apologize in advance because this imagery is quite graphic. When you vomit, have you ever collected the vomit and eaten it? What do you think that Jesus would do with the vomit? Would he collect it and put it back in his body or would he toss it far away from him?

Many people teach that a Christian can't lose their salvation, but what would you do if you vomited? Would you keep the vomit and put it back into your body? If we're the Body of Christ, what happens if you become vomit? You have to think about that question. You have to think about James 4:4a, which says, “Adulterers and adulteresses, don't you know that friendship with the world . . . makes him (you) an enemy with God” (NKJV). You have to seriously ask yourself this question. How many enemies of God go to heaven? How many enemies of God does he allow into heaven unless they repent and change their ways?

Of course, everyone on earth is allowed to go to heaven if they change their ways and walk as Jesus commanded. Will people be accepted in heaven if they are blatantly serving the world? I'll let you ponder this question. I would suggest that you think about it quite seriously.

I'm not going to give you the answer. However, if you've paid attention in these last two chapters to what I’ve written about not serving the world and coming out of the world and the lukewarm church, I suggest that you make a change.

Chapter 6
Loving in action

Let me start with a scripture passage in 1 John 3:16-18 (NKJV).

"By this we know love, because He laid down his life for us. And we also ought to lay down our lives for the brethren. But whoever has this world's goods, and sees his brother in need, and shuts up his house from him, how does the love of God abide in him? My little children, let us not love in word or in tongue but in deed and in truth."

It's one thing to say that you love God and people. It's quite another thing to become someone who has such a reputation of loving in action that someone who can't pay their power bill or who can't afford groceries can come to you and ask you for money to pay their power bill or buy food.

Do you honestly exude that much love and compassion in your life? Do people approach you and tell you that their power will be cut off unless they pay their bill and ask you to help them?

Do you walk in such love and understanding that a woman could approach you and say that her husband gambled all of their money away, so she needs to feed their children for the next week? Would you give her some money? Do you walk in that type of love? Do you even mix with people who have these kinds of needs?

Do you know that many people in the U.S. where this book will be released don't have homes? People walk past them and ignore them, like the priest and the Levite did in the parable of the Good Samaritan. (See Luke 10:25-37.) They walk on the other side of the road and don't even acknowledge the homeless person.

Do you have this world's goods and see your brother in need and shut up your heart from him? If so, how does the love of God abide in you? (See 1 John 3:17.)

Do you see homeless people in your city? Do you shut up your heart toward them?

Have you ever asked a homeless person if he'd like a drink of Coke? Have you ever asked a homeless person if you could buy him something to eat? Have you ever asked a homeless person if he needed $5? Have you ever even acknowledged the homeless person in your midst?

Do you flow in such love and understanding that people would actually approach you and share their needs with you? Are you free with your money and led by the Holy Spirit so that you can hear the Holy Spirit tell you, "Give that person a $100"?

Matthew was led to ask a friend of his today for their PayPal address so that he could send them $100. They didn't ask for the money; they just shared that they had a need.

Will others share their needs with you, or do people think that you don't even care? By this we know God. By this we know love because Jesus laid down his life for us. We ought to lay down our lives for the brethren. (See 1 John 3:16-20.)

Are there people in your church who are not doing too well? How would you even know? Do you mix with people who aren't doing well? Those people might have jobs, children, cars, and houses, but they aren't doing well. Are you there for them? Do you even hear the cries of the needy?

Jesus demonstrated his love for us by dying on a cross for us. He gave everything that he had. Will you go without this week to feed someone who needs money? Will you go without when you see a need? Will you spend your money on the needs of others? Do you even care? Do you care more about your brands, your cars, your houses, your possessions, and what your friends and family think of you?

Of course, giving to a homeless person or giving to someone whose husband has gambled away their money causes judgment from friends, other people, and family members. They might judge you for giving to someone with a gambling addiction. They'll judge you for giving to a homeless person. Many people don't give to the poor simply because they fear the reaction of their friends and family.

Who do you fear more? Do you fear God, or do you fear your friends and family? Many people are reacting and not acting in love because of this fear. What would happen if Jesus had not overcome his fear in the Garden of Gethsemane? What would have happened to all of us if he had not gone to the cross? What if his fear had conquered him? Where would we all be? You have to ask yourself these hard questions.

Jesus demonstrated his love for us by laying down his life for us. The way to conquer the world and its lusts is to think of other people, those that need to be saved. Think of others for whom you could buy a book because they need to be trained better in the Christian faith. Think of other people that could be really encouraged by a Christian ministry that you know. Think of someone that you could support and help publish their book. Think of others. Stop spending on yourself. Stop thinking about yourself. Stop concentrating on yourself.

Turn around. Make a turn around. Make a change. Repent. Turn the other way. Make a difference in this world. **Be** the difference in this world.

If you see injustice happening, step in and address and conquer the injustice. It's one thing to say that you are Christian. The word *Christian* means *little Christ*. Are you really being Christ to this world? Are you demonstrating Jesus Christ to others? Think about that. Do you need to make changes? I suspect your answer is yes.

CHAPTER 7
The faithful ones

Let's shift the pace. What if you had little money? What if you had little strength or little ability? What if you didn't have much power or knowledge? What if you gave the little that you did have to the Lord? What if, in your little understanding, you read a book like *The Parables of Jesus Made Simple: Updated and Expanded Edition* by Matthew? What if you read all those parables, and you set a goal for yourself to obey them all and live them out in this world?

What if you took them apart and studied them and did them? What if you read a book on the commands of Jesus and learned to obey them? What if you didn't have a whole lot, but you did what the Lord said? You would be faithful.

Revelation 3:8 says, "I know your works. See, I have set before you an open door, and no one can shut it; for you have a little strength, have kept My word and have not denied my name."

The faithful Christian, the faithful church, the faithful believer understands what Jesus taught and obeys his words. "That have kept my word," Jesus said in Revelation 3. He tells the church that they just have a little strength, but they've kept my word. If you read Matthew's books, you probably realize that he speaks a lot about the commands of Jesus. You might not know that I repeated, "If you love Jesus, obey his commands," six times in my writings.

The very idea of the commandments of Jesus seems weird and is not understood by most Christians. If you ask the average Christian what the commands of Jesus are, they might say, "Obey God and love him with your all your heart and love your neighbor." Well, they might not love God when they serve the world because they're serving the world rather than God. According to James 4:4, they're being an adulterer to God.

They might not love their neighbor when they spend all of their money on themselves, and they don't care about other people that need to be saved. They spend all their money on serving themselves and gaining possessions because of their own pride.

They deny their neighbor and don't share the message of salvation with others. They don't use their money wisely to disciple others or fund ministers to send them to spread the Gospel. They don't love God, and they deny their neighbor. The average person knows these two commands but does not follow them. Even so, there are at least fifty commands of Jesus.

Many people don't understand these commands. Here is a link to the fifty commands of Jesus in the Kindle book.

If you are reading the paperback version, search Google for "the fifty commands of Jesus," and you'll find them.

The passage in Revelation says, "You have little strength, but you've kept my word," which means you've obeyed the parables and the commands of Jesus, "and you have not denied my name." That means that you not only obeyed Jesus, but you didn't deny him.

When he told you, Matthew, to do things like write a series of books from saints from heaven, you didn't deny his name. You didn't deny his direction. You didn't deny the fact that Jesus sent you to do those things and told you to do them.

Also, dear reader, if you are put in a situation where you are asked if you are a Christian and you could come under persecution for saying that you are a Christian, you need to admit that you are one. Someone in the workplace might have heard you make a comment about homosexual marriage or former President Obama or Hillary Clinton. They might be unhappy about what you said, and they asked you, "Are you a Christian?" If you answered, "No,

I'm not," and you actually are a Christian, you've denied Jesus's name. Christians might have little strength and might not have a lot of earning capacity or potential. If they have not denied the commands of Jesus and have never denied the fact that they're a Christian, then they are faithful Christians.

Verse nine says, "Indeed I will make those of the synagogue of Satan, who say they are Jews and are not, but lie—indeed I will make them come and worship before your feet, and to know that I have loved you."

In this passage, if you take the word *Jews* and change it to *Christians* now because that's who the people of God are, you can see that some people who worship in normal churches aren't real or authentic even though they claim God as their God and Jesus as their Savior. He will make those hypocrites who serve the world and who are part of the lukewarm and religious church come to you in humility and acknowledge that Jesus really loves you as a true Christian.

At one point, these people were mocking you. They were saying that you were off track, too extreme, and too passionate about Jesus. However, later on, Jesus will make them come and repent to you and say they're sorry and admit that Jesus loved you.

Does Jesus love them? Well, there are different forms of love.

John 14:21 says, "He who has My commandments and keeps them, it is he who loves Me. And he who loves Me will be loved by My Father, and I will love him and manifest Myself to him."

Doesn't God love everyone? Why does Jesus say that those who obey his commands will be loved by him and by his Father? Don't God and Jesus love everybody?

Well, there seems to be different levels of love for God with higher and greater forms of love. This is a higher grade of love that is talked about here. The Christians of the religious churches, the lukewarm Christians, will come and bow down and acknowledge that Jesus loves these people more. He seems to love them more than they are loved by Jesus themselves.

"Because you have kept My command to persevere, I also will keep you from the hour of trial which shall come upon the whole world, to test those who dwell on the earth" (Revelation 3:10). When the tribulation happens, these faithful ones will be supernaturally preserved and protected from the effects of the marketplace and the trouble and tribulation of those times.

Just as Noah passed through the judgment in the ark, so will these faithful Christians pass through the judgment and be supernaturally protected by God. Do you want to be a faithful Christian, or do you want to be a lukewarm Christian who serves the world and is an enemy of God?

CHAPTER 8
Losing your first love

Here is some encouragement for some of you. You might be not serving the world. You might not have the most expensive car but just have a basic car. You don't have the fanciest house. You don't have a lot of money. You truly do your best to serve God. You like to read and understand scripture. You like to go to church and research teachings on YouTube. You read books and do your very best.

Even so, my message has convicted you. You are convicted about not serving the world, and you think that you can do better in some ways. You are convicted about having need of nothing and about being lukewarm. You don't want to be vomited out of Jesus's mouth.

When I talk about looking out for the needs and desires of others and laying down your life like Jesus, you are convicted. You believe that you could have been a better steward with your money. When I talk about giving to ministries and supporting one of Matthew's books, you are convicted and can see your need for change.

You're not a bad person. You can really feel what I'm saying. You've been convicted to change. Revelation 2:2 might apply to you.

"I know your works, your labor, your patience, and that you cannot bear those who are evil. You have tested those who say they are apostles and are not, and have found them liars."

Isn't that true today? Many people are calling themselves apostles. Verse 3 continues, "And you have persevered and have patience and have labored for My name's sake and have not become weary."

You've done works for God and served him. You've done the best that you can. Even through all the trials, persecutions, hassles, and struggles in life, you haven't grown weary. You're doing your best.

Verses 4 and 5 say, “Nevertheless I have this against you, that you have left your first love. Remember therefore from where you have fallen; repent and do the first works, or else I will come to you quickly and remove your lampstand from its place—unless you repent.”

When Jesus was talking to the whole church about this, he's saying that he was going to remove that church from being a church unless they repented.

This might mean that things won’t end well for an individual believer unless they repent. Now, repent doesn’t mean that you become a Christian. Repent means that you turn around and make a change. Why do you have to make a change? What's Jesus talking about here? What did I write about here in Revelation?

You have left your first love. It says, “Remember therefore from where you have fallen; repent and do the first works, or else I will come to you quickly and remove your lampstand from its place—unless you repent.” Turn back around to Jesus and do your first works. What were your first works?

Well, many people are saved. They are brought to Jesus and are excited. The Holy Spirit starts to make changes. He says to you, “Don't drink so much. Don't do this. Start to give to the church. Start to attend church. Start to change your behaviors.” When someone is saved, their friends often become Christians too because of the radical change in their life. It's so evident that the best time for you to ever reach your friends is when you've had an encounter with Jesus, and you've just been captured by this love affair with him.

What happens? Well, religion and false teaching sets in. All sorts of traditions of men set in. Soon enough, you start to compromise. You might say things like, "It's okay not to give to those homeless people. It's okay not to give to the wife of a gambling husband. The husband will just take advantage of us if we give to his wife all the time and feed his kids. He should stop gambling, or he should be ejected from the church."

This person might start to lose his love of God. He starts to lose this love of his fellow brethren. You move away from Jesus. You're trying your best, but you're not as close to Jesus as you first were. You might need to change.

If you think this could be you, you might benefit from the following books that Matthew wrote:

- *7 Keys to Intimacy with Jesus*
- *Finding Intimacy with Jesus*
- *Jesus Speaking Today* and
- *The Parables of Jesus Made Simple: Updated and Expanded Edition*.

These books would help you come back to Jesus and will turn you around. *Influencing your World for Christ* will also help you get back on track with your Christian faith. *Finding Your Purpose in Christ* will teach you how to live your life and pursue and fulfill your destiny so that you can become who Jesus wants you to become.

You just need to turn around and come back to God. Refine a couple of things and make some changes in your life as you are led by the Holy Spirit. Change the things in the previous chapters about which you were convicted. Change your spending habits and your attitude toward the things of the world. Change your attitude toward what you think about who you are and what your friends and family think of you. Start to become a radical Christian again.

Desire to see other Christians grow and be radically transformed by Jesus.

Pursue intimacy with Jesus and return to your first love. Obey Jesus and his commands and parables. Support other ministries that teach Christians how to be Spirit-filled and how to live their lives to the fullest potential. Support missions and outreaches for people to be saved.

Will you turn around? Will you change? Will you do what I tell you to do?

We're almost finished with Matthew's questions. I am just going to address one final portion of the book of Revelation: the Jezebel spirit and her effect in society.

CHAPTER 9
Don't tolerate Jezebel

In this chapter, we will talk about not allowing the Jezebel spirit to have any influence. The scripture in Revelation 2:19-23 tell us,

"I know your works, love, service, faith, and your patience; and as for your works, the last are more than the first. Nevertheless I have a few things against you, because you allow that woman Jezebel, who calls herself a prophetess, to teach and seduce My servants to commit sexual immorality and eat things sacrificed to idols. And I gave her time to repent of her sexual immorality, and she did not repent. Indeed I will cast her into a sickbed, and those who commit adultery with her into great tribulation, unless they repent of their deeds. I will kill her children with death, and all the churches shall know that I am He who searches the minds and hearts. And I will give to each one of you according to your works."

The last sentence is very sobering. "I'll give to each one of you according to your works." Jesus is saying that he's going to repay people according to what they have done. Now, the beginning is very positive. "I know your works, love, service, faith, and your patience. As for your works, the last are more than the first." He continues, "Nevertheless I have a few things against you because you allow that woman, Jezebel, the prophetess to reach out and seduce my servants." Other versions say, "You tolerate that woman, Jezebel."

If you're called to be a prophet like Matthew is, you'll have many confrontations with people with a Jezebel spirit. Many people have a calling of God as a prophet, but Satan also knows that they are called. Many times, Jezebel will trap a prophet in sexual immorality or even through genetics and generational curses with a demon of Jezebel.

Many people who are called as prophets will have a Jezebel spirit in them, and they need to be healed and delivered. Matthew has had a Jezebel spirit a couple of times, and he's had to repent and be delivered of that spirit. He actively saw the spirit leave and his prophecies and his behavior change.

Mentioned in 1 Kings 16:31 and other passages, Jezebel is the woman that served as the queen of Israel with King Ahab. Ahab was a weak king, the king of Israel, but he bowed down to his wife and served her. A typical Ahab-Jezebel relationship might look like the marriage of Bill and Hillary Clinton. Bill Clinton is Ahab, the weak man that bows down to his wife. Hillary Clinton is currently one of the most wicked Jezebels on the face of the earth.

If you love Bill and Hillary Clinton, you really won't like what I just had to say, but the Jezebel spirit is very seductive, cunning, and deceptive.

Jesus warns the churches not to tolerate or allow someone with a Jezebel spirit to operate in their church. People used to eat foods sacrificed to idols, and Jezebel tempted them to do it. Jezebel might not tempt you to commit every sin, such as have sexual relations outside of marriage or commit fornication or adultery. Jezebel can have you serve yourself and take control of your own destiny so that aren't submitted to God. You might have an adulterous relationship with God, serving idols and even yourself instead of serving and submitting to him. Jezebel often walks in rebellion and is full of pride, control, and manipulation.

I recommend the following excellent book on the spirit of Jezebel by Bill Vincent: *Destroying the Jezebel Spirit: How to Overcome the Spirit Before It Destroys You!* This great book will give you a solid understanding of the Jezebel spirit, how he or she operates, and how to detect, avoid, and defeat it.

The issue that Jesus had with these people is that even though they did great works and even though their last works were greater than their first works, including service, faith, and patience, they allowed evil, wicked prophets and prophetesses and those with Jezebel spirits to operate and influence the church, even in leadership positions, positions of power that influenced the church.

The Jezebel spirit isn't confined to the church. Many people with Jezebel spirits operate in the media, in Hollywood, in government, and in politicians. The Jezebel spirit is a controlling, manipulating, prideful, and rebellious spirit. However, they come across as sweet, demure, and loving. It is not restricted to women although it has a female name. Men can operate in this spirit as well.

Like Hillary, they might say, "I've had such a hard life. The election was stacked against me. Everything went wrong. Russia interrupted. Trump was so shocking; he came out of nowhere. He shouldn't have won. It was terrible. Everyone conspired to make me lose. People made false accusations against me. The FBI destroyed my candidacy. Everything was against me." This is the language of a typical Jezebel: poor, poor me.

Whenever we tolerate this spirit or allow it to dominate, Jesus is not happy. Jezebel has to be taken out of power so that she stops influencing the church. This is who Jesus was talking about. Many Jezebels hold high titles. They might be on the worship teams or even be pastors, prophetesses, or prophets in the church. Pastors sometimes are intimidated by them and even feed into their schemes. A pastor is in disobedience if he knows someone with a Jezebel spirit but doesn't remove them from their office or position of power or leadership in his church.

I really recommend *Destroying the Jezebel Spirit: How to Overcome the Spirit Before It Destroys You!* It's the best book that Matthew has ever read on the Jezebel spirit. Like any resource that I suggest in this book, I don't recommend it just for fun. I suggest it for further reading and further instruction for you. This is the end of Matthew's questions. We'll go on to Sheldon’s questions next.

PART 2: SHELDON'S QUESTIONS

QUESTION 1
Power to become a son

This is section two, question one and is taken from the book of John 1:11-12. "He came to His own and His own did not receive Him. But as many as received Him, to them He gave the right to become children of God, to those who believe in His name."

Sheldon observed that some translations say that he gave them the *power* to become the sons of God, not the *right* to become the sons of God. Sheldon wondered if John could please explain more about this power to become sons of God or this right to become the sons of God.

I'd like to say that many children have been raised to really honor their father. People use the expression, "Well, he is a real son of his father." When a son really does a tremendous job, he brings glory, praise, and honor to his father. However, some sons are so disgraceful, so disobedient, and so rebellious that they bring their father dishonor.

In one aspect, you can say that we're all children of God. God loves everyone in the world and through Adam, we all become children of God. However, a son is someone who has been accepted as an heir, someone with a special position with the full authority that comes with the inheritance that belongs to a son.

The son of a wealthy billionaire walks in the power and stature of his father. He commands respect and authority. You only have to look at Donald Trump's sons, young Donald or Eric. They walk in great authority, power, and dignity. They bring so much honor to their father.

A popular cliché on earth states that the apple doesn't fall far from the tree. Another expression says that children are really showing the fruit of the father. The father might be a great person.

Through his children, he proves that he is a great father, and his children prove that they are really sons of the father.

We have covered that many people are saved, but they become lovers and friends of the world, disobedient adulterers and adulteresses. Some of these children of God, who are accepted and saved through Christ, never really reach their full potential or a place of intimacy with Jesus that they are capable of.

Of course, if you are lukewarm and you are vomited out of Jesus's mouth or if you become a friend of the world and an enemy of God, who does that make you? Are you actually a son of the Father? Are you going to inherit the Kingdom of God? Are you going to inherit the full power and anointing of the Father?

It's a right, a privilege to be called a son of God. It's a powerful exchange. Jesus takes the sinfulness of men, and through the waters of baptism, he renews the person into becoming the righteousness of Christ in God.

The miracle of the new birth and the new creation is that old things pass away. Rather than being the child of the devil or a child of wickedness, you become a child of righteousness. As Romans says, instead of your members performing with disobedience, your members start to obey the rule and the government of righteousness in your life.

I consider it a great honor to be accepted as a son of God. People are realizing that they don't have to call themselves a pastor, prophet, teacher, apostle, or evangelist. They can fully realize their power and potential simply in identifying themselves as sons.

A son of a king is a prince, and the prince walks around with the authority and the inheritance of the king. A son of a billionaire walks around in the authority and the preeminence of their billionaire father. You can see this modeled by Ivanka Trump. Even though she is a woman, she is still a son of God. Eric and

Donald display wonderful examples of who the sons of God are meant to be.

I hope that I helped you understand more about identity. It's a real privilege and an honor to be a son, and this should not be treated lightly or with disdain. No prince should be involved in drunkenness, nude parties, orgies, or any other despicable behavior. A prince shouldn't be dressed with his shirt unbuttoned to his belt, have pink hair, look weird, or act strangely. A prince should bring honor to the king by how he carries himself and the way he behaves. As sons of God have been adopted into the royal family of God, you should act accordingly.

A royal exchange happens when we become a son of God along with the related rights and privileges. Many people are saved in this world but never really come to realize or live out their potential and power as a son of God. The Father is looking for sons in this hour who can demonstrate the power and influence of heaven on earth.

Response from Sheldon

This is such a beautiful answer. I love the way John so thoroughly covers the attitude of one who is a true son and how that relates to those going through the maturing process. They have to come to a mindset of their true nature of their personhood and sainthood as real born-again children of God. People who actually have the Spirit of God can feed others that are also coming into the kingdom while still living their earthly existence. They have received his words in the good ground of their hearts, allowing it to grow to fruition,

The entire born-again experience to maturity is quite a process. The almighty God himself gives us the great opportunity and honor of adequately manifesting the image of Christ as he is fully formed in us. I am glad that John exemplified this in his walk on earth and gave us the books he did along with this interview from the kingdom side of eternity. He is one of my favorite Bible authors, and his writings have provided a great foundation to learn to love and keep the faith through all the hard times we go through in our lives. He is probably one of the greatest examples of Christ being **fully formed** in someone.

The subject of having the power/right to become the sons of God is what the Bible is really all about. As God's bride in the Old Testament, Israel provides an example of instruction for the people to love God and their brothers and sisters in the society that God established. Christians now have not only the opportunity to become members of the Bride of Christ, which relates to intimacy, but also to become sons of the most high God, speaking in authority and godly exemplary relationship. This opportunity should not be squandered with carnal mindedness, self-glorification, and pride. The Holy Spirit is concerned with weeding these attributes out of us.

I asked this question to help people see salvation not just as something that happens in the sense of a born-again birth but so that they can note the process and mindset that this produces in the true child of God as we grow from gloriously experiencing God in salvation through each of the stages to maturity as nurtured sons and daughters of God. When I share having the kingdom within, I tell potential new members of the kingdom about their heart as the manger of Christ. There is no place for Jesus in the world, and as they walk and grow, they are taking Jesus with them through everything they do. If you wouldn't take your little brother to do something, consider the same for Jesus as he grows in you to be fully formed and as you manifest his life in this world.

QUESTION 2
The disciple Jesus loved

The second question that Sheldon asked is, "Why did John describe himself as the one that Jesus loved?"

We spoke earlier about John 14:21. I'll share that with you here, and we'll read it and go through it. This verse says, "He who has my commandments and keeps them, it is he who loves Me. And he who loves Me will be loved by My Father, and I will love him and manifest Myself to him."

Now, we also spoke earlier about those who received him (the Jews) and that they have the right and the power to become the sons of God. It's commonly accepted that Christians are considered sons of God, but not all of them are walking in that sonship or understand their identity. Not all of them are walking worthy of their calling or their destiny.

Many Christians walk around and behave as if they're orphans without a real father in heaven, without the rights, the ability, and the authority of the son of God or the son of the king.

Although John 14:21 might seem controversial, the passage says, "He who has my commandments and keeps them, it is he who loves me." Who loves Jesus? Who is Jesus saying loved him? The people that know the fifty commandments and the people that obey those fifty commandments. They are the people that love him, the people that obey what he taught.

He taught in Matthew 7:26-27: "But everyone who hears these sayings of Mine, and does not do them, will be like a foolish man who built his house on the sand: and the rain descended, the floods came, and the winds blew and beat on that house; and it fell. And great was its fall."

Jesus is saying that the wise man here is the person who builds on the rock of the teachings of Jesus. The foolish man is someone who disobeys the teachings of Jesus. Jesus is saying that his commands are central to and a big part of loving God. The way that you prove that you love Jesus and that you demonstrate your love for him is by obeying his commands. If you're going to be disobedient and lust, crave, envy, and be jealous, along with doing many things that deprive God and your neighbor of love and honor, you're not really loving Jesus or obeying him.

I was the person that Jesus loved because I was obedient. I understood him and took the time to do so. Because I took the time to love Jesus and obey him, he really loved me. I wrote six times in my writings, "if you love Jesus, obey him" (three times in John and three times in my letters).

John 14:21b says, "And he who loves Me will be loved by My Father, and I will love him and manifest Myself to him." God and Jesus have a certain form of love for people here, which is another level. He has a special love for people that are obedient.

Jesus's love is like any teacher who loves his favorite student. He loves the student that runs after everything he teaches, that reads all the assigned and even the suggested books. When the teacher suggests further reading material, the top students will read all the suggested books and will have a lot of questions. That student will dialogue back and forth with the teacher.

The way you prove that you're a good student is by obeying the teacher and reading the extra resources, just like I've quoted these resources by Matthew. In this way, you really prove your love and your interest in this subject by not only reading the assigned book but by going on to read the suggested books given as resources.

I obeyed Jesus and taught people to obey him and to demonstrate their love by laying down their life. Jesus loved me with this extra special love because of my obedience and my understanding of what he taught.

In Matthew 7:24-27, Jesus tells the parable of the wise man who built his house on the rock. This person hears his teachings and obeys them. You only become a great student by following in the footsteps of your teacher. You only ever become a rabbi by sitting at the feet of a rabbi, learning from him, and then practicing what he taught. Finally, you go on to teach what he taught. I not only sat under the teachings of Jesus, but I obeyed and demonstrated them. I started to walk as Jesus walked.

1 John 2:6 says, "He that says he abides in Him ought to walk just as He walked." I didn't just write a scripture. I meant it and lived it out. I demonstrated Jesus on earth by walking and acting like him and doing signs and wonders like him because I was so obedient to what he taught. I was such a practiced student and obedient lover of his, so Jesus loved me. That was why I even said in my gospel that I was the one that Jesus loved because a special form of love is found in intimacy. If you don't have that intimacy or special form of love, you might hear Jesus say, "Depart from me, I never knew you."

I not only obeyed Jesus and carried out what he taught, but I taught what he taught. I went on to teach the fifty commands of Jesus and more and teach and equip people how to obey and walk in the Holy Spirit so that they can obey the commands of Jesus. I was loved by Jesus for the person that I was going to become after he left the earth.

Response from Sheldon

Wow, there is no lack of conviction in all of that. After all, I asked the question. As we all know, the grace of God carried Peter through his sifting, and I expect that to some degree, John had to deal with sifting as well. The more that one adheres to the commands of Christ, the easier that the process of refining is. Since John wrote most of the commands of Christ for us, we can expect that he learned them as well. We all are going through the process of learning to walk in the Kingdom even while we have to live in the carnal world, which is constantly testing us and our faith. Reading this as John has provided makes me think of the verse where Matthew, Luke, and Mark all record ". . . Who then can be saved . . . " and Jesus's answer to them and to all of us is "With God, all things are possible."

Through the grace of God, we actually make it through life's struggles and move into the heavenlies and do good to others in need. This is how we even survive the evils of the world where mediocrity abounds and at every turn, mandates of righteousness are watered down in our legal systems and in governments around the world. The systems of the world call for excellence in your studies and in your participation at work, in sports, and in the military, yet they lack the moral compass to lead in our spiritual lives and society itself. Keep Jesus and his commands close to you and meditate day and night on them so that you can pass every test the world throws at you and obey them with boldness to truly be the light and salt as representatives of the Kingdom of God in the earth.

I have personally gone through much consternation as an intercessor for the unsaved as it seems they won't make it. The Spirit of intercession has the same heart attitude to those that are perishing that Jesus and our Heavenly Father has for them—that they would come and ask for God help since it is readily available and that they too would believe in his great sacrifice on the cross for all of us. Truly, Christ will draw all men to himself as this was his promise for us on the cross; we were all on his mind. Oh, that we would have him securely seated in our thoughts and hearts so that we could show him and his glory to others who so badly need to taste and see that God is good and not end up vomited out of his mouth.

Love the Lord with all your heart, soul, mind, and strength, and he will honor you, and his glory will shine upon all your comings and goings so that others might know that he is good by what they see in your life. (See Matthew 5:16.)

QUESTION 3
My experience on Patmos

Sheldon's question is: "What was it like being exiled on the island of Patmos?"

I want you to understand that I'm often referred to as the apostle of love and people know me as the person who preached and shared on love. As we just covered, I was the apostle that Jesus loved, and I wrote in my gospel that Jesus loved me.

As I said, I wrote six times in my letters and in my gospel that if you say you love Jesus, you should obey him. This is part of demonstrating your love for him.

1 John 2:6 says, "He who says he abides in Him ought himself also to walk just as He walked." If you say that you have an abiding relationship with Jesus, a close and intimate relationship with him, you should behave accordingly and do what Jesus did and said.

Because I loved God so much, I loved people as well. Part of obeying Jesus is demonstrating and carrying out his love for them, treating them with compassion, courtesy, patience, kindness, goodness, and all of the fruit of the Spirit flowing through you. Part of my experience in Patmos was sadness. I really cried that I was taken away from my church and exiled. I couldn't communicate with the people of God whom I dearly loved.

I was like an overseeing apostle and a bishop for them. It was just like a leader or a shepherd being taken away from his flock, so he worries, and he's concerned. You notice that the apostle Paul mentioned that he not only suffered all these hardships but that he also suffered with concern for his flock and for the people that he was teaching.

Part of a shepherd's heart is to invest his life, time, and prayers into the people that he's leading and guiding. A shepherd's anxiety and struggles are often found in the things that are facing his flock that he wants to lead them out of, such as self-deception. Instead, he wants to lead them into truth or into being a more effective and a more powerful Christian.

The exile to Patmos took me away from people that I loved, which was very sad. It's not only sad to be away from society, but when you love people and when you're full of the love, compassion, and understanding of Jesus, it's hard to be taken away from the object of your love—the people of God.

Part of the exile to Patmos was also ecstasy because I didn't have a lot of food, and I often didn't sleep very well. A combination of not having a lot of food and not sleeping well sent me into like a fasting state. This prepared me spiritually for radical encounters with God. Revelation records that I received the vision of what is in the book of Revelation while I was on Patmos. I saw and heard things of the future. I visited heaven in that current time, and I visited the earth in the future. I saw the future past the thousand-year millennial reign of Jesus. I've not only seen the future when I was in Patmos two thousand years ago, but I've seen the future in heaven as it's played out.

I've seen all the books that Matthew will ever write, and I've brought them down into his living room today to show them all lined up. I know the future. I did have the vision of heaven and the encounter that made up the book of Revelation.

When I was at Patmos, seeing the vision for the book of Revelation wasn't my only spiritual encounter. I was engaging with the angelic realm, God, Jesus, and the Holy Spirit. I was engaging with saints in heaven that had gone from paradise below the earth to heaven when Jesus resurrected. I was engaging with the angels and the saints of the Bible. I was engaging with visions of God and taking other trips to heaven. I was living a life of ecstasy and spiritual bliss.

There was a real bliss about it because I was taken away from the trappings of the world and from the carnal life with the world. I was taken away from trying to get by in the world and fight the flesh and put down the flesh man. I really had focused on these exceptional experiences with the Kingdom of God and the supernatural lifestyle of God.

On one hand, I suffered because I was away from the people of God, the object of my love, those who I dearly loved. But on the other hand, because I was away from them and because I had so much time with little food, I was caught up in a continual spiritual ecstasy with trances, visions, and all sorts of radical encounters.

Some people today are speaking of heavenly encounters and going to the courts of heaven and having visions of angels and saints. Matthew's had a pretty radical life, but all of those experiences pale into insignificance compared to what I experienced on Patmos. I was not only dearly loved by Jesus, but I was treated to a travel fest through heaven. The people of heaven, the angels of heaven, and God, Jesus, and the Holy Spirit came to make a habitation on earth with me. I was greatly impressed, supported, and highly encouraged. I didn’t feel desperate, as if I were going out of my mind. But I quite literally was called totally out of my mind by some in the religious church because I was living such an extraordinary Christian supernatural lifestyle.

I hope you liked that answer.

Response from Sheldon

What can I say but that this chapter is sobering yet a blessing at the same time? Many of us have gone through dire straits and suffered, and by crying out to God, we know how he changes our prison and brokenness into a shrine of his glory. He does this to the extent that you can walk around barefoot even with the scorpions and snakes of the world all around, and nothing will harm you or even come near to you. Many of you can relate to that. When you are in that place, it leads you to the arms of God himself.

Through all our troubles and all our tears and the experiences that break us, God is there through it all, holding us. He is truly able to succor us and keep us going, for he knows the end of it all just as he knows the beginning.

John gave us the actual book of the Revelation of Jesus Christ, which shows all that will occur to bring the complete restoration of God's rule in the entire universe and all levels of the spiritual realm. Our God will meet you and reveal himself to you.

God will give you the love and grace to go through to the end as he did with John and millions of others since, including this little broken man and my dear friend Matthew, who is allowing God to use him to write these books.

Perhaps you will be encouraged as you one day go through your own encounter. God is ready to reveal himself. The tribulations and traumas we go through are used by his Spirit to bring us through the torn veil to the very mercy seat of God where we will be surrounded by his angels and introduced to the great cloud of witnesses who arrived in heaven before us.

Thank you, John, for your kindness to visit us and make sense of the things we get to go through.

QUESTION 4
Other things Jesus said and did

Question four of Sheldon's is based on John 21:25. "And there are also many other things that Jesus did, which if they were written one by one, I suppose that even the world itself could not contain the books that would be written."

Sheldon's question is, "If Jesus said and did lots of things that weren't recorded in the Bible like that passage says, what are some specific examples of those things?"

The first thing I will say is that Jesus took all of the apostles out one day in a boat to walk on water. We all know that Peter walked on water, and he sank, but Jesus picked him up, and then Jesus and Peter walked back to the boat on water again. That's not recorded in the Bible, but that's what actually happened.

It really doesn't make sense for Jesus to pull Peter up and then drag him through to the water back to the boat while Jesus walked on water. Dragging him through the water doesn't make sense, but that is how many readers imagine that it went down. One thing that's not recorded in the Bible that actually happened is Peter walking back to the boat on water.

The lesson from that is that Peter walked on the Word of God when Jesus said, "Come." The actual word *come* gave Peter the ability to walk on water. Peter walked on that command, and the water actually became solid underneath his feet so that he could walk on it. Jesus walked on water, and as he placed each foot in the water, the water became solid like an ice cube.

The lesson that you can learn from that is that Peter walked on the very Word of God, the command of Jesus, and then on the way back, he walked hand in hand with the Word of God. John 1:1 states, “In the beginning was the Word, and the Word was with God and the Word was God” (KJV). Jesus has been the eternal Word of God, so, in the first instance, Peter walked out on the Word of God, and in the second instance, Peter walked on the water, hand in hand with the living Word of God back to the boat.

Another day, Jesus took us all into the boat, and all of us got out of the boat and walked on water. It was amazing because some of us in the boat that saw Peter walk on water wished that we had been brave enough to try as well. A couple of us even talked about it to each other and said, “That was amazing. I wish that I had gotten out of the boat too because I would've walked on water.”

Jesus heard our thoughts, and one day, he surprised us. He took us out fishing and then taught us all how to walk on water. We were able to do signs and wonders because there's nothing like walking on water to increase your faith.

Additionally, Jesus used angels just like people can do today in the glory realm. He often used angels to deliver people. He didn't need to individually lay hands on people to cast out demons but multiple times in crowds, he actually sent out angels to do deliverances and healings on people. That's not mentioned in the Bible, and people might even object to that. They might have an issue with that, but Jesus did it.

Jesus knew how to command angels, and we were able to see the effects that angels had and how they ministered with him and worked and co-labored with him in the harvest. At some points in Jesus's ministry, the crowds were so large that it took four or five of us healing people also. People just flooded in and flocked to us. Thousands of people came from other nations, following us.

It was like managing a tent city, a whole flood of people who were desperate to be healed. Many times, six of us disciples were laying hands on people and healing them. Jesus taught us to minister, command angels, and have angels work with us to help with the healing and the deliverances of the people.

The Jewish people are tremendously generous, so people were always coming to Jesus and giving money and alms to him as a rabbi and to us as his followers. We had an abundance of money coming in. However, people were always coming to us who were short of finances and money, so we gave out the money just as fast as it came in.

Judas never managed a large amount of money because as fast as it came in, it went out. Many Christians don't understand that Jesus had a lot of people giving him money. They tend to have issues with money and don't listen to what Jesus said in Matthew 10:5-8 when he told us that we should give freely since we received freely. They have issues with those in ministry taking money, being given money, and being supported by other people. However, Jesus was not only supported by common people, but Mary Magdalene and other rich people came and gave of their wealth to him.

Acts recorded that the early church was built on the finances of people who sold houses and all their possessions because they found something greater—the pearl of great price. They traded in everything they had to possess it. This lifestyle of giving is largely forgotten by the modern church.

Response from Sheldon

I knew this would be an amazing chapter. They all are, but it's wonderful to hear more details about what we have read in the Bible and see a little more behind the curtain, so to speak, and learn what else happened in these instances of the Kingdom of God invading the culture of John's day. What a taste of heaven on earth! We will get to hear more stories in greater detail of what happened that was not yet recorded in the Bible when we spend the first ten thousand years in his glorious Kingdom.

Currently, some authors have taken up this mantle and written novels, including historical stories by Max Lucado and Taylor Caldwell, to name only a couple. You can read some very encouraging and inspired books, but these will pale in comparison to the books that could be written by people meeting with those in the cloud of witnesses and recording and sharing their interactions with Jesus on earth. This is just one way that some could use to bring more of the Spirit of God and his loving and caring ways to readers of books and blogs so that heaven invades earth. Technology is vastly increasing the ways to spread information to people and even connecting them for collaboration on projects.

How does God want to use you to facilitate heaven invading earth as it happened John's day? The books that Matthew and others have written will give you some examples. What moves your spirit? What excites you? Who would you like to interview or commune with in heaven, besides Jesus and your Heavenly Father? You can speak to all those who have passed and who have been through such horrendous and amazing things. Everything written in the Bible that the men of God went through is for us to see that the works of God are available now on earth as easily as they were in their day. Imagine a world full of books on all the lives of everyone who ever lived; this library already exists in heaven. God wants to see other things in heaven come to earth. Have you not heard that God gives witty inventions as recorded in Proverbs 8:12? He is waiting on people who are intimate with him to get the breakthroughs they need so that they can steward these things to be designed and made on earth. They will bless all of mankind and bring others into the kingdom of light. After all, inspiration is light.

QUESTION 5
Raising Lazarus

Sheldon's fifth question is, “What was it like to see Jesus raise Lazarus from the dead?”

This was a great question. What do you do? Jesus had already raised the boy that was in the funeral procession from the dead. He had also raised Jairus's daughter from the dead. People had been raised from the dead in Jesus's ministry two times as recorded in the gospels. Here is a story that’s a follow up to the question, “What are some of the stories not recorded in the Bible?”

Jesus raised quite a few more people from the dead than just those two examples. He was the greatest miracle worker that the world had ever seen up until that time. A person really has to be on top of the game to do greater things than what Jesus did. He was a remarkable person with tremendous abilities, and no one was more submitted to the Father than Jesus Christ.

The difference with Lazarus's miracle was that Lazarus was closely connected to the Pharisees and well respected among the leadership of Israel. He even had Pharisees attend his funeral. He was quite important and wasn't just the son of a synagogue leader. He wasn't just part of a funeral procession like the other recorded miracles. He was highly respected in Jewish society.

The Jews believed that a person could be raised from the dead within three days of their death. They believed that the spirit of a person hovered around the body for up to three days. But on the fourth day, the spirit departed, so the person would never be raised from the dead.

This common Jewish belief stated that it was impossible to come back after four days. Jesus delayed going to heal Lazarus until he died so that we didn't arrive until the fourth day when, according to Jewish lore, someone couldn't be raised from the dead. He delayed, which Mary and Martha didn’t understand. They wondered why Jesus didn’t come sooner, and they were upset and cried.

They didn’t realize that Jesus was setting himself up to be killed and crucified, so he needed to do a dramatic miracle at this time. He came to Lazarus's death, and he said that he was the resurrection and the life. He called Lazarus forth from the tomb, and Lazarus walked out in his grave cloths, which is symbolic of us in our dirty grave cloths of sin being resurrected into a new life in Christ.

Lazarus came forth. Jesus had done the impossible, which totally rocked the Jewish world at the time. The Pharisees had been at the funeral, and they knew how long Lazarus was dead. There was no denying it and no stopping the rumor that Jesus did something spiritually and doctrinally impossible. That was a mighty sign. The Jewish leaders decided that it was expedient that one man should die so that the whole Jewish nation would not perish from an uprising (John 11:50).

Jesus was close friends with Mary, Martha, and Lazarus. He stopped at Lazarus's house many times when he went to Jerusalem. As his disciples, we didn't understand why Jesus didn't go straight to Lazarus when he heard that his friend was sick. Jesus had time for strangers and had helped tens of thousands of people that he didn't know and had no relationship with, but when his friend became sick, he delayed and went somewhere else.

We had no understanding, no comprehension of what the Holy Spirit had planned. We even wondered and asked Jesus why he wasn't going to heal Lazarus and were really concerned for their friendship.

After Lazarus’s resurrection, the family held a great celebration. Martha wasn't concerned about Mary sitting at Jesus's feet and didn't stress about what had to be cooked or prepared.

Instead, she was overcome that her brother was raised from the dead. They could not contain the joy that was in their house that day.

They so loved their brother, the man of the family, the leader of all the staff on the property, and the person in charge. Their life was put into disarray when they lost the main breadwinner of the family. On the other hand, his resurrection was a great day of celebration in that house. However, Jesus put a nail in his own coffin when the Pharisees decided that he was too much of a threat to the system. They no longer wanted him to walk around, telling the people that he was the Messiah. He was now doing the impossible and raising people from the dead on the day after it was doctrinally allowed.

Jesus had finally done something that not only embarrassed the leaders but proved that there was mistruth in the essential, foundational beliefs of Jewish culture. It was an exciting day, but this day turned out to lead to the death of Jesus on the cross.

Response from Sheldon

I can imagine that you had to be there to truly experience what happened but to have it described from this perspective in Jesus's ministry is astounding.

The trauma and glory surrounding that whole ordeal must have been one of the most glorious moments in Jesus's ministry as he made an open show of his power over death. The kingdom of darkness thought that it had one-upped God by wielding the fear of death, but Jesus just walked in and made a mockery of death. The teachers of the day that held power over the people of God with fear of the curse of death were astounded.

I expect Satan and his children were experts at causing men to fall into a premature death due to the curse of the law and even push them headlong into activating such curses in the Old

Testament, such as Balaam and Balak (Numbers 22-24), who brought a curse upon the nation of Israel. Satan has used such tactics ever since.

We have to really thank God for the cross, and by simply coming to his seat of mercy through the rent veil, we can see that these curses will not succeed in our own lives as we repent of chasing after lust, pride, and even power over others. "Oh vanity, vanity, all is vanity" (Ecclesiastes 1:2, loose paraphrase), I can just hear Solomon say. The enemy of God and all his vanity is mocked before the entire world, and the day will come when all the world will see it happen again. Satan, his evil minions, and the kingdom of darkness will ultimately be vanquished, and the gates of hell will shrink into nothingness as they are destined to the lake of fire with all those who refused the love of God and accepted the devil's lies. They sold out to hell for their own fame and glory.

In 2 Peter 3:9, we see that God is not willing that any should perish but that all should come to repentance; that's the Gospel, folks. Repent— turn around—and see that God is good; even death bows to his will. If you are in Christ, the kingdom of darkness and the gates of hell will have to bow to you as well. Bring those that God shows you as the love of God arises in your heart, bring them into his great and glorious light as his ambassador.

QUESTION 6
Confidence to witness to others

Sheldon's next question, number six is based on this verse, 1 John 4:18. "There is no fear in love; but perfect love casts out fear, because fear involves torment. But he who fears has not been made perfect in love."

Sheldon's question is, "If love casts out fear, why are so many Christians bound with fear and scared to evangelize? What do you have to say about how to evict fear from Christians so that they can evangelize?"

People have many fears. One of the key frustrations that many Christians face is that they do not have any supernatural evidence that Jesus exists. They don't feel that they have a powerful enough testimony to bring someone to salvation. We covered this early in the book when I talked about people storing up possessions out of pride and that they want to show off and be accepted and respected as someone with a nice house, the latest car, well-behaved children, and brand-name clothes. People like to be revered and highly respected by their friends, co-workers, and family. They don't want to be looked down upon or seen as weak, ineffective, and helpless.

Many Christians fear the repercussions of opening up and sharing that Jesus is the answer and that he can solve your problems and that you need to accept him or you won't go to heaven.

They fear losing their job, losing friends, and not being accepted. So many people allowed Jezebel to reign in the church and in society, controlling and manipulating them because they fear losing friends. They fear losing the person with a Jezebel spirit as a friend. They fear an uproar or a confrontation. There's so much fear in the world. Sheldon's question is, "How do you overcome this fear?"

First of all, you need to be hopeful that you can develop the ability to do something supernatural. Healing might be a challenge for you to learn. Praying Medic has written a book called *Divine Healing Made Simple*. He has two other books of testimonies of healing that you can read after you have read the first book: *My Craziest Adventures With God – Volume 1* and *My Craziest Adventures With God - Volume 2*. These books share testimonies of his healings, which will give you faith for healing. You might even want to follow his example and learn to heal and then lay hands on people. That certainly brings results so that people agree that there really is a God. They cannot deny the results after they see something painful in their body totally disappear because you prayed for them.

Many people don't progress in a healing ministry because they fear rejection. They fear failing in healing. They feel that if they try and heal someone and it doesn't work, they'll be embarrassed. They don't want to be embarrassed if the person isn't healed.

You might want to read a book on visitations of hell that people have experienced. You have to come to a point where you understand that if people aren't saved, they will go to hell. One of the ways to develop your ability to love in a greater way is by growing close to Jesus. You can get to know him better by reading *7 Keys to Intimacy with Jesus* by Matthew. Read that book and apply it so that you grow in your intimacy to such a place with Jesus that you become living love, a portal of love that walks around the world.

You can also read Matthew's book, *Prophetic Evangelism Made Simple*, and receive and develop the gift of prophecy. Everyone that he has prayed for has received the gift of prophecy. Practice it and learn to approach people and give them prophetic words, which will rock their world and give them a supernatural and miraculous encounter. This will help convince even skeptics that there is a God and that something supernatural is happening.

Many people have a fear of witnessing because they are concerned for their reputation, of losing a job, or of losing possessions or money. They need to know Jesus better. They need to understand his love for people better. They then need to develop that form of love so that they can receive the mind of Christ and consistently obey his commands so that they start to have Jesus manifest his mind and heart in them so that they think like Jesus and seem like him to people.

When people can actually feel as Jesus did, when they can supernaturally feel Jesus's emotions for others, this love will compel them to step past the fear and not worry about the consequences and witness and practice evangelism with their friends.

Matthew wrote another excellent book, *Influencing Your World for Christ*. In the book, he practically describes how he lives out his life by acts of love, compassion, encouragement, and by generally just being salt and light in his community so that he can win people to Christ.

So much fear is bound up in thinking that you have to share the gospel and win a person to Christ the first time that you talk to him or her. People think that if you don't win a person to Christ the first time that you share with them, you fail. So few people realize that people often need seven to ten encounters with the gospel before they're converted. When you speak to someone, you're just one encounter of those seven, and you probably are not the one who will lead the person to Jesus.

If you take the pressure off yourself to save a person and if you just focus on sharing love and being love to people, then you can still impact them. If you drop the belief that you have to save them and just encourage and love people without an agenda, this takes the fear from doing it and opens up opportunities through the Holy Spirit so that the person asks you specific questions that will lead to their conversion. This is explained in more detail in *Prophetic Evangelism Made Simple* and *Influencing Your World for Christ*, both written by Matthew.

Response from Sheldon

Thank you, John. A huge "thank you" to Matthew and the others mentioned in this chapter. If you read all the books mentioned in this chapter and focused your spiritual life around them for six months, you might just start walking on water yourself. I have read some of them and need to read them again and prayerfully put a concerted effort into getting back into this phase of my life.

The Holy Spirit is the Spirit of boldness. We can only see any results in breaking away from the fear that the world sows and that wants to permeate our flesh by the power of the Spirit. I would personally rather soak in the anointing of Jesus and be pickled by it instead of swallowing the world's counterfeits that are politically correct and non-offensive. When you're speaking in love as moved by the Holy Spirit, the only spirits that are really offended are those that keep people in darkness and delusion and in bondage to their spirit of fear.

Do you really want to see the best reward in heaven? If so, let your brother, sister, mom, dad, friend, boss, neighbor, co-worker, and anyone you come in contact with see God at work in and through you. This is the only way they will come to know him is through one of seven to ten encounters that they need. God is faithful as you sow his Word in their lives. You're sowing Jesus and his love for them.

Stay out of arguments and just say, "Let me show you." They will agree, which opens the door for authority to kick in at that moment. I know a nine-year-old boy that did this. He told his friend, "I will pray and fast this weekend, and God will take that scar away from your arm." Sure enough, the scar disappeared that weekend. That boy woke up amazed and accepted Jesus into his life the next time he saw his friend. It really is that simple—not only come to God like a little child as this boy did but approach those you wish to witness to with this same spirit and attitude.

Don't argue. Instead, move past this with *Prophetic Evangelism Made Simple*, one of Matthews's books. Remember, God wants to not just tell the person about his love, but he wants to show it to them. Ask them if you can pray for them and their loved ones that might be ill or sick or influenced in any way by the kingdom of darkness. See God move. He always honors this type of ministry.

QUESTION 7
Walking in the light

The seventh question from Sheldon is based on 1 John 1:6. "If we say we have fellowship with Him and walk in darkness, we lie and do not practice the truth."

Sheldon wonders what it means to walk in darkness. What does it take to walk in the light? People say that they have fellowship with God, but they still walk in darkness. Why do people have fellowship with God but still walk in darkness?

One of the keys to this question is the word *lie*. If we say we have fellowship with him and walk in darkness, we lie and do not practice the truth.

The answer to this question is found in 1 John 2:4. "He who says, 'I know Him,' and does not keep His commandments, is a liar, and the truth is not in him."

A person who says that they love Jesus or knows Jesus yet does not obey his commandments is a liar, and the truth is not in him. You might be a Christian who invited Jesus into your heart; you might go to church; you might attend Bible studies, you might say one-way prayer with Jesus and God; you might read your Bible, but you still walk in darkness.

I say pretty clearly here that a person who says he knows Jesus and does not obey Jesus's fifty commandments is a liar, and the truth is not in him.

The key to walking in the light is knowing the commandments of Jesus and walking in them. Truth is found in the parables, in the teachings of Jesus, and in walking in them. If you say that you know Jesus, then you should be doing what he taught. If you say that you are a follower of Jesus, then you need to walk in his footsteps. If you say that Jesus is your teacher, then you need to be a willing student and do what he teaches. If you say that Jesus is your Lord, then he should be your master, and you should be doing what he tells you to do.

You can be a son and still be subservient to your father. You can be a prince and still do what the king tells you to do. You can still come under authority as a son of God.

People walk in darkness when they don't love their brother. "He who says he is in the light and hates his brother is in darkness until now. But he who loves his brother, abides in the light and there is no cause for stumbling in him" (1 John 2:9-10).

The person who says he's in the light and hates his brother is in darkness until now. However, there is also is a person who says he loves Jesus but doesn't obey his commandments, which are the practical outworking of how to love your brother.

If you say that you are a Christian and that you love and know Jesus, you should obey his commandments. If his commandments are the practical outworking of how to obey Jesus, then you need to follow and do the commandments. If you're not walking in the commandments or obeying what Jesus taught when it comes to dealing with other people and God, then you don't love the other people. You might say that you love them, but you're not acting in love or demonstrating love.

He who loves his brother abides in the light with no cause of stumbling in him. Another way to interpret verse ten is: "He who obeys the commandments of Jesus abides in the light with no cause of stumbling in him. If you are obeying the commandments of Jesus with the understanding of how to treat and how to love your brothers, if you're walking in the commandments, then you'll always love your brothers. If everything you say and do is what Jesus taught you to do, then you'll always act in love.

The apostle Paul says, “Walk in the Spirit, and you shall not fulfill the lust of the flesh” (Galatians 5:16). The way to walk in the Spirit is to obey the commandments of Jesus and the directions of the Holy Spirit. The only way you can obey the commands of Jesus is by drawing on his strength and ability in the empowerment of the Holy Spirit.

When you’re continually asking for help and the abiding presence of God through the empowerment of the Holy Spirit, you grow used to calling out to the Holy Spirit. You are used to living a life through his power and enablement. You become proficient at being led and activated by the Holy Spirit and walking with him.

Galatians says that when you walk in the Spirit, you won’t fulfill the lust of the flesh. This includes all the sins mentioned in Galatians.

The way to walk in the Spirit is to obey the commands of Jesus and what he taught. When you obey the commands of Jesus, you’re not a liar. If you say that you have fellowship with him and walk in darkness, you lie and do not practice the truth. The way to walk in the light is to abide in Christ, and the way to abide in Christ is to obey his commandments.

1 John 2:6 says, “He who says he abides in Him ought himself also to walk just as He walked.” In other words, the person with a great relationship with Jesus walks, talks, and acts like Jesus. I could do that and behave that way because I was so close to Jesus and was obedient to him. So I acted and behaved like Jesus everywhere I went. I walked in the light.

Many Christians are walking in darkness because they have no idea what Jesus taught and what he meant when he taught the Sermon on the Mount along with his other teachings. If you don’t have the list of the commandments of Jesus, go back to that link and look them up along with the scripture references. Start to walk these out. Print out the list of the commandments of Jesus, put them on your fridge, and start to obey them. Until you obey them, you are not living as well as you could. In fact, if you don't obey the commandments, then you are a liar, according to 1 John 2:4.

This is the time when you need to read this, turn around, and start to act and behave the way that Jesus taught you.

Response from Sheldon

All I can say to respond to that deep truth is let it go deep. The deeper it goes within you, the deeper it will plow the spiritually lazy parts that are in all of us.

In my own darkness, Jesus met me, and he will meet you too. He will minister to you and show you how to carry on and even use you and your story to impact the lives of others.

I studied much of the Bible in my twenties and participated in evangelism, and God used me in little ways. I will know more about this in the long run when I hear about those affected in heaven. But in my thirties, all I had was him. The church that I was helping in my twenties turned out to be graceless and bordered on a cult. I had participated in their beginnings with my misplaced religious understanding and my own darkness, thinking I was wise. I found folly in pushing things ahead and assisting God in his timing. With God, you truly get what you sow.

In my forties, after the murder of my twenty-one-year-old son, all I had left was Jesus. In my brokenness and my darkness, he lit a fire for me in the Spirit and sowed the truth of his kingdom in me. He showed me how the kingdom really works through many encounters with ministering angels and probably saints, not only ministering to me, but this entourage affected the lives of others as he paraded me around, showering me with his glorious love and light and moving in and through my heart. I was able to see how the kingdom is shown and sown through compassion and how the Holy Spirit lives in our hearts and reaches out from there to affect the lives of hurting and needy but receptive people.

I recall one vision I had during this time of going back and seeing the apostles walking down the street with their shadows healing people. I had read about this in the Bible. Then I saw their shadows healing people in the vision, not black or dark but a bright white light even brighter than the ambient surrounding light. When I contemplated what I was seeing, I came to understand that this is what seeing the fullness is all about with both the spiritual and the physical interacting. Let your darkness be invaded by God's light and love. Walk with him awhile and taste and see that doing Jesus's commands is not burdensome but that they bring the greatest rewards—souls affected for the kingdom, including yours as well.

QUESTION 8
Final words

Sheldon's last question is based on 2 John 12. "Having many things to write to you, I did not wish to do so with paper and ink; but I hope to come to you and speak face to face, that our joy may be full."

Sheldon's question is, does John have something that he'd like to say to us face to face now?

Well, we have come to the last question in this book, so I will share my final words.

If you lived or had an office that was a stone's throw away from a cliff, and people were blinded and walking past your office straight off the cliff, dying, would you leave your office every time you saw one of these blinded people walking by? Would you go out and stop them, shake them, and say, "I know you're blind. You need to walk the other way." Would you turn them around so that they wouldn't fall to their death? Would you warn them?

Or would it be more loving of you to sit in your chair and say, "Well, they're going to die one day. They might as well die today. I'm not going to be bothered to get out of my chair and keep on warning these people. They're blind. They're going to their death."

What's more loving? Is it more loving for you to get out of your chair every time you see one of these people and turn them around and set them on the right path, or is it more loving to just say that it's not your business to correct them as you have a job to do that doesn't involve saving lives? You're in the office chair. It's your job to save lives.

By and large, the church is sadly being led by blind guides. This is one of the most serious books Matthew has ever been part of. He doesn't recall if any of his books have ever had so many messages that call for repentance. If you've read this book and think that it was a good book and if you felt convicted in your spirit, it's your job to warn people.

People are being led by blind guides. They are blind. I hope that many of the things in this book have been a revelation to you. The Jezebel spirit might be lying to you or trying to control you. The blind are now leading the blind just as Jesus warned. Many of the things I've shared with you are fundamental to me and to Matthew. However, the average Christian doesn't see or understand these things.

It's not okay to sit in your office and watch people dying and going to hell. It's not loving of you. Spending ninety-nine cents to read *Influencing Your World for Christ* in three hours should be a priority for you. Most people aren't interested in evangelism because it threatens them. They might be embarrassed about it or lose their job or a friendship, but sadly, most Christians don't want to get out of their office chair and disturb their life.

The average Christian isn't really concerned about sharing the gospel and the good news of Jesus Christ. The only people they seem to be concerned about are their personal friends and their family. Many Christians are religious and bound up with legalistic teachings of an angry God. They have shared this negative impression with their family and friends, who have rejected the message. These people would desperately like someone to come alongside their friends and family and save them. You can be that person.

I have many things to say. I said quite boldly in my gospel that I was the disciple that Jesus loved. Other disciples, other people heard what I said. They wanted to know why I was so special. I told you that I could abide and do everything that Jesus taught and did. I did signs and wonders. I walked on water. I raised the dead. I healed cripples. I grew out legs. I saved people from lame situations. I made the blind see and the deaf hear. I did miracles, signs, and wonders everywhere I went. I oversaw a tremendous movement of God.

I was very successful. I received great rewards in heaven, but it's just such an honor and privilege to come down here and speak to you people and share a very serious message with you. It's such an honor to come down and say, "Hey, you are walking past my office; you're headed for destruction. You're blind. Hey, you, reader, listen to me. You're walking toward danger. I have gotten out of my chair in heaven. I have come from eternity to warn you, shake you, turn you around, and point you in the other direction."

What do you do when you read those chapters and feel convicted? You need to make a change. How are you going to make the change? You're going to read the resources and go and do what I've told you to do.

It's no use saying, "I'm sorry." It's no use saying, "Well, he's beating up on me." It's no use saying, "Who does he think he is, saying that I'm blind?" I've come down from heaven. I've been here, speaking through Matthew for hours.

As you're reading this, I'm watching you. What are you going to do? Are you going to finish reading this book over and say, "Well, that was interesting?" Or will you make changes and repent?

To repent is to turn around. Change your direction. Make a 180-degree turn. Many of you are walking off a cliff. You're blind and headed for destruction. These are scary words. It is time to make your peace with God and set your life in proper order.

Are you a light in this world? Are you shining the light of Christ brightly? When people meet you, do they meet Jesus? When people meet you, do they understand that there's something different about you, something that stands out, something that they want? When they meet you, are you an extraordinary person to them, or are you just another person of the world that preaches a religion that you don't practice?

Do you actually see anything that needs to change in your life? Are you convicted about anything? Has the Holy Spirit used what I've said today to touch your heart? Are you struggling because you've lost your first love, and you need to be restored? Maybe you need to read the following books so that you can get to know Jesus and God better:

- *Finding Intimacy with Jesus Made Simple*
- *Jesus Speaking Today*
- *Conversations with God: Book 1* or
- *Conversations with God: Book 2*.

You might need to have a two-way conversation with Jesus or God and read *How to Hear God's Voice: Keys to Two-Way Conversational Prayer*.

You might want to know how to influence your world for Christ. You might consider buying, *Influencing Your World for Christ*. You might want to know what the parables actually mean and what Jesus taught so that you can live them out and apply them to your personal life today. You might need to buy, *The Parables of Jesus Made Simple: Updated and Expanded Edition*.

I hope that my words have touched and encouraged you. I plead with you about these serious issues. I hope that you will forgive me for coming out of my office, grabbing you by the shoulders, and saying, "turn around." God bless.

Response from Sheldon

It's very hard to follow up after all of that. Read over these words a few times. You might want to read this book monthly or even weekly for a while and let the Spirit of such conviction and wisdom become your best friend. It might just change your life and turn it around or even turn it upside down. Maybe everything you are doing now will bring earthly rewards, and maybe you want to shift now and invest in more heavenly rewards. Perhaps you have had enough of the mediocrity of the grind of the machine from living a life not totally focused on bringing the Kingdom of heaven to earth.

John notes how he is honored in heaven and about the movement of God on earth. He had a great role of stewarding this as one of the leaders who followed Jesus. This is not something to compete with or try to be one up on. What I am simply saying is that the world has seen what some men filled with God's presence and guidance can do with not only revivals but even in homes that were coming apart at the seams. His Spirit came in to turn things around and bring light and love where there was only darkness, strife, and evil. Everything you have gone through up until now has prepared you for the conviction of this book. Reading the other books mentioned in these pages as resources will give you an awesome understanding and practical steps that you can incorporate into your life to truly see the kingdom come and God's will being done on earth as it is in heaven. Selah.

I'D LOVE TO HEAR FROM YOU

One of the ways that you can bless me as a writer is by writing an honest and candid review of my book on Amazon. I always read the reviews of my books, and I would love to hear what you have to say about this one.

Before I buy a book, I read the reviews first. You can make an informed decision about a book when you have read enough honest reviews from readers. One way to help me sell this book and to give me positive feedback is by writing a review for me. It doesn't cost you a thing but helps me and the future readers of this book enormously.

To read my blog, request a life-coaching session, request your own personal prophecy, request a visit to heaven, or to receive a personal message from your angel, you can also visit my website at http://personal-prophecy-today.com All of the funds raised through my ministry website will go toward the books that I write and self-publish.

You can also request a trip to heaven with Robin Gann.

To write to me about this book or to share any other thoughts, please feel free to contact me at my personal email address at survivors.sanctuary@gmail.com

You can also friend request me on Facebook at Matthew Robert Payne. Please send me a message if we have no friends in common as a lot of scammers now send me friend requests.

You can also do me a huge favor and share this book on Facebook as a recommended book to read. This will help me and other readers.

HOW TO SPONSOR A BOOK PROJECT

If you have been blessed by this book, perhaps you might consider sponsoring a book for me. It normally costs me between $1,500 and $2,000 or more to produce each book that I write, depending on the length of the book.

If you seek the Holy Spirit about financing a book for me, I know that the Lord would be eternally grateful to you. Consider how much this book has blessed you and then think of hundreds or even thousands of people who would be blessed by a book of mine. As you are probably aware, the vast majority of my books are ninety-nine cents on Kindle, which proves to you that book writing is indeed a ministry for me and not a money-making venture. I would be very happy if you supported me in this.

If you have any questions for me and what projects I am currently writing that your money might finance, you can write to me at survivors.sanctuary@gmail.com and ask me for more information. I would be pleased to tell you what projects I am currently working on.

You can sow any amount to my ministry by simply sending me money via the PayPal link at this address: http://personal-prophecy-today.com/support-my-ministry/

You can be sure that your support, no matter the amount, will be used for the publishing of helpful Christian books for people to read.

OTHER BOOKS BY MATTHEW ROBERT PAYNE

The Prophetic Supernatural Experience

Prophetic Evangelism Made Simple

Your Identity in Christ

His Redeeming Love- A Memoir

Writing and Self-Publishing Christian Nonfiction

Coping with your Pain and Suffering

Living for Eternity

Jesus Speaking Today

Great Cloud of Witnesses Speak

My Radical Encounters with Angels

Finding Intimacy with Jesus Made Simple

My Radical Encounters with Angels- Book Two

A Beginner's Guide to the Prophetic

Michael Jackson Speaks from Heaven

7 Keys to Intimacy with Jesus

Conversations with God: Book 1

Optimistic Visions of Revelation

Conversations with God: Book 2

Finding Your Purpose in Christ

Influencing your World for Christ: Practical Everyday Evangelism

Deep Calls unto Deep: Answering Questions on the Prophetic

My Visits to the Galactic Council of Heaven

The Parables of Jesus Made Simple: Updated and Expanded Edition

Great Cloud of Witnesses Speak: Old and New

Walking under an Open Heaven

A Message from My Angel: Book 1

Interviews with the Two Witnesses: Enoch and Elijah Speak

Gaining Freedom from Sex Addictions: Breaking Free of Pornography and Prostitutes

Mary Magdalene Speaks from Heaven: A Divine Revelation

Princess Diana Speaks from Heaven: A Divine Revelation

How to Hear God's Voice: Keys to Conversational Two-Way Prayer

You can find my published books on my Amazon author page here: http://tinyurl.com/jq3h893

Upcoming Books

Conversations with God: Book 3

ABOUT MATTHEW ROBERT PAYNE

Matthew was raised in a Baptist church and was led to the Lord at the tender age of eight. He has experienced some pain and darkness in his life, which has given him a deep compassion and love for all people.

Today, he runs a Facebook group called "Open Heavens and Intimacy with Jesus." Matthew has a commission from the Lord to train up prophets and to mentor others in the Christian faith. He does this through his Facebook posts and by writing relevant books on the Christian faith.

God has commissioned him to write at least fifty books in his life, and he spends his days writing and earning the money to self-publish. You can support him by donating money at http://personal-prophecy-today.com or by requesting any of his other services available through his ministry website.

It is Matthew's prayer that this book has blessed you, and he hopes it will lead you into a deeper and more intimate relationship with God.

www.ingramcontent.com/pod-product-compliance
Ingram Content Group UK Ltd.
Pitfield, Milton Keynes, MK11 3LW, UK
UKHW020139250726
13967UKWH00002B/745

9 781973 211198